ROOSTER CALL

RISING UP TO MANHOOD
THROUGH SPIRITUAL LEADERSHIP

PAUL GOOD

Carpenter's Son Publishing

Published by Carpenter's Son Publishing, Franklin, Tennessee

Published in association with Larry Carpenter of Christian Book Services, LLC of Franklin, Tennessee

Cover Design by Armando Vera

Editing by Nesbitt Creative

Interior Layout Design by Adept Content Solutions

ISBN: 978-1-946889-01-0

Printed in the United States of America

CONTENTS

III

The only thing necessary for the triumph of evil
is for good men to do nothing.

Edmund Burke

A real man is one who rejects passivity, accepts responsibility,
leads courageously, and expects the greater reward, God's reward.

Robert Lewis

CHAPTER 1

TWILIGHT'S SHADOW

Shadows loomed large from the last few rays of light streaming behind the hills of the Judean countryside as the sun slipped into the Mediterranean Sea. The serene, comforting sound of bleating sheep and goats from the flocks below was disturbed by the sensual giggles of a man and woman from the large tent on the elevated landscape, where lingering smoke ascended from stone altars. Moments later a young Jewish woman emerged from the side flap door, looking disheveled and frantically tucking her hair back under her veil. After retying her belt she hurried off down the dusty road before anyone could notice her. Inside the rear of the tent were two men, Hophni and Phineas, sons of the high priest, Eli, lounging on ivory couches and reaching for the table next to them arrayed with fruits, vegetables, baked goods, wine, and fresh roasted lamb.

Suddenly the backdoor flap was flung open, and the aged Eli stormed in! "My sons, what are you doing?"

Startled by the sudden intrusion and a lack of sobriety, Hophni jumped up from his couch and dropped his cup of wine onto his robe.

Eli continued, "Since you have taken over for me as priests for the sons of Abraham and Israel, the reports coming back to me are not good! They're not good! I hear you take for yourselves the people's sacrifices that are allocated for God, and you force them to offer more than they intended to give. You're sloppy and careless in the offerings, and I hear you're sleeping with the volunteer women attendants! You are degrading the name of God! It's gone on too long! You must stop."

"Easy, old man," the older Hophni replied, wiping off his wine-drenched robe. "Don't get up on your righteous high horse now. You've been getting a lot of the benefits, too! Every day we bring you roasted prime rib of lamb with all the fixings and the best wine the Ephraim has to offer. Then there's that nice big bag of gold now and then. . . . And I haven't heard any complaining until now!"

"What's this all about?" Phineas piped in, grabbing a handful of pistachios off the table. "You know this is the way we've been running things since you left. Chill out!"

"It's wrong, boys!" Eli insisted. "And besides, last night a prophet visited me, and he said God is not pleased—judgment is on its way! He says you're both going to be killed and our family line abolished from the priesthood."

Hophni laughed. "Who will kill us? We're the priests! Nobody can touch us. You've been drinking too much wine, Pops! Nothing's gonna happen! Go back to Mom and play with the grandkids. We got this under control."

"Yeah," added Phineas, "we got it, Pop. Here, take this new wine and fresh loaf. And don't listen to these wacko seers who show up needing a bath."

"No, I'm serious!" Eli said with urgency. "I believe this was a true man of God. It's coming! Judgment is coming!"

"Pop, we're handling things just fine. We're making the offerings; don't you worry." Phineas put the wineskin in the trembling, wrinkled hands of the old priest, turned him around, and walked him out the door. "Good night. *Shalom!*"

Phineas watched as Eli walked away shaking his head. Then a young female worship attendant appeared, coming back from the creek. She was carrying the cleaned pots and utensils used for the sacrifice. He called out to her, "Hi, hon, what's your name? Come over here for a minute."

★★★

Although a bit modernized, a scene similar to this must have taken place during the dark days of the judges in the nation Israel around 1080 BC, after God brought them out of Egypt and placed them in the promised land for about three hundred years. The father, Eli, the high priest for the nation, had retired for the most part, and his sons had taken over managing the tabernacle and handling the sacrifices for Israel. But they were corrupt, abusing their position and power with no respect for the Lord, the sacrifices, the worshippers, the women attendants, or the nation as a whole. In fact, all they cared about was themselves and making sure any lust or passion in their hearts was fully satisfied.

Eli had lost any influence or control over them. He had not instilled the necessary awareness of the reality of God in their lives. He did not teach them the importance of living in a way that honors God. Quite ironic, especially since they were priests in the ministry and were supposed to teach others about God and the way to God! Eli had forgotten the great proclamation by Joshua, who had led them into the promised land and said, "As for me and my household, we will serve the LORD" (Josh. 14:15, NIV).

It wasn't long after the prophet warned Eli about the abuses and coming judgment that tensions again built up with neighboring Philistines, who kept trying to take back their territory. Finally war broke out. Hophni and Phineas joined the fight, bringing the ark of the covenant from the tabernacle to the battle to ensure they had God's presence and blessing for victory. But they were greatly overpowered by the Philistines and the ancestors of Goliath so that thirty thousand Israelite soldiers fell. Among the dead were Hophni and Phineas, and the ark of the covenant was captured.

A messenger ran to tell Eli, and upon hearing the news that the ark had been taken by the enemy, fell backward off his chair, broke his neck, and died. In addition Eli's descendants and relatives who would have rightfully inherited the priesthood were killed a short time later also. With the captured ark, the glory of God and his visible presence vanished. The tabernacle shut down, and Israel's enemies retook land. Everything that defined who Israel was had departed. It was disaster of monumental proportion.

Why? What was the root cause of this calamity? It was because a man, a father who was supposed to be a spiritual leader, dropped the ball and didn't fulfill his calling. A man failed to instill a respect for God to those under his care and lost his influence to get them to turn from wrong to do what was right. Notice the prophet came to announce a warning of judgment to Eli, the father.

This short story that opens 1 Samuel in the Old Testament and took place approximately 3,000 years ago is loaded with application and extremely relevant for us today. Most corruption and evil that exist in our world, wreaking havoc and disaster on ourselves, on our families, and our communities, stem from the lack of spiritual leadership by men. That's the cold, hard truth. Men all over are not stepping up and fulfilling the role of overseeing and influencing others in the way of goodness and honoring God, just as Eli failed with his sons. Even though outwardly the priests held high positions in their society, they hurt many in the end, including themselves.

Does this not reflect what is happening in our world today? We look pretty good outwardly, all-important with successful careers, nice homes, social status, and even active members at church, but what's our true spiritual state? What kind of effect are we having in our God-ordained role as spiritual leaders? Are we making an impression on others to walk with God and showing them how? Too many of us men have dropped the ball in our responsibility to become a spiritual leader and guide those under our care and sphere of influence in the way of truth. I include myself, and I'm in ministry! Look around: has not the curse been especially seen in our land of late due to our passivity and being taken up with our own desires and purposes, over and above this important responsibility? We're in a spiritual twilight, with the awareness of God's presence and any accountability to him fading fast!

Recent Barna Group research shows that the United States is confused about the difference between right and wrong: biblical morality is being escorted out and, as Barna President David Kinnaman writes, "a new morality of self–fulfillment—with the goal to enjoy life as much as possible" is being ushered in. Pew Research Center also recently conducted a survey of 35,000 people showing that roughly 71 percent of Americans identify with Christianity; this is down 8 percent from the last survey taken seven years earlier. Most alarming, only one-third of Millennials (those born from 1982 to 2002) identify with any kind of faith.

Additionally, there's a divorce in America every thirteen seconds with almost 40 percent of children, grades one through twelve living without a father or father figure. As a result, 71 percent of all girls experiencing teenage pregnancies come from fatherless homes, as reported by US Department of Health and Human Services. National Principal's Report found 71 percent of high school dropouts come from fatherlessness homes as well. Additionally, the National Center for

Fathering states, "Even if you are an involved dad, until we are successful in *correcting this epidemic,* our children and grandchildren will be growing up in a culture of absent fathers and unfathered children. *And they will be affected"* (emphasis added).

Most of us know these disturbing statistics of which I've barely scratched the surface. But it's not the president or current administration's fault, it's not schoolteachers' fault, it's not technology's fault—men, it's our fault. When we fail as spiritual leaders to influence others to live for God's purposes, our societies are the worse for it. Believe it or not, that's our number-one job as men and our main purpose while here on earth! We're to lead in the way of right and wrong, goodness, love, honor, kindness, justice, and everything else that make up the character of God, especially with our families.

When Adam and Eve fell in the garden by disregarding the ways of God and eating the forbidden fruit, a curse came all over the land. You'll notice God called out to Adam. Even though Eve made the initial choice, he was the one responsible!

Of course we like to pass the blame and responsibility to others, just as Adam did. But the truth is, we're responsible.

You may agree with the downward spiral of society but say, "What can I do change that? What can one man do?" It begins with accepting and reclaiming the position of spiritual leader ourselves and inspiring other men to do the same.

★★★

The term *spiritual leadership* can sound elusive and mysterious, a bit out of reach, but it's really not too complicated. It's knowing the way to live to honor God in order to experience his presence and blessings through a relationship with him and his son Jesus Christ.

I like to think of it as being a God guide, guiding others to the phenomenal life of walking with God. Oswald Sanders, in *Spiritual Leadership,* defines this leadership role as "the power to change the atmosphere by one's presence, the unconscious influence that makes Christ and spiritual things real to others."

But we're not going to lead anyone to honor God with their life or influence them to walk in his presence until we first learn to ourselves. If we're living with unrestrained passions, according to our natural desires that are constantly aroused by the world's messages, the last thing on our mind is the presence of God. We're running in the opposite direction from him!

But when we seek God, wanting to know what it takes to honor him and be near him, we live our life in a certain way, warding off any evil influences that might keep us from experiencing him and his blessings. That's how we get on the path to become a spiritual leader.

This is the rooster call: to rise up out of our slumber as irrelevant men to live lives that glorify God and teach others around us to do the same.

God needs men to wake up, put away their deeds of darkness, and arise to be men who have the courage to walk in the light of God's truth and then declare it to others, awakening them from the deadness of night to live accordingly to that light—like a rooster. God needs roosters!

Roosters are pretty spiritually significant with Christianity. They came to be identified with Christ's passion since the crowing marked Peter's denials of Christ. Later in church history the rooster signified the resurrection, as well as the repentance of the saints and religious vigilance. When a rooster crows it's warning off any harmful predators that might come to devour the roost. This is why they are seen on weathervanes atop churches and houses: they are symbolic of watchful vigilance against evil.

It's the perfect symbol for spiritual leadership for us guys. It doesn't hurt also that John Wayne and later Jeff Bridges played the bold and tough Marshall Reuben "Rooster" Cogburn in the epic film *True Grit*!

Using the acrostic ARISE as a guide, over the next chapters we'll cover five fundamental areas we need to focus on continuously in order to reclaim our masculinity through fulfilling our God-given role as spiritual leaders. Our world is constantly male-bashing, as we'll see in the next chapter. Manhood has lost its glory and luster in our Western society, and it's directly related to our lack of genuine spiritual leadership. When we recover our position as spiritual leaders, our dignity and respect as men will return! E. M. Bounds said, "The church is looking for better methods; God is looking for better men." With courage let's take the challenge, have some laughs along the way, and become the men we were made to be. It will bring glory to God and great blessing to us and our loved ones, our churches, and ultimately our world.

A.R.I.S.E.

A—AFTER GOD'S HEART

Man's chief end is to glorify God, and to enjoy him forever.

Westminster Shorter Catechism

Years ago manhood was an opportunity for achievement, and now it is a problem to overcome.

Garrison Kellor

Man is a good thing spoiled.

Saint Augustine

CHAPTER 2

RUBBING OFF THE TARNISH

In 1996 a tragedy occurred on Mount Everest. Four separate expedition teams set out from base camp early in May that year, when weather conditions are usually the mildest and most ideal for climbing. After a few people reached the summit, a fierce storm, uncharacteristic of the season, rose up suddenly and made their descent virtually impossible due to high winds, snow, and zero visibility. Two men were late to leave the summit and were forced to remain near the peak overnight; others were caught in the storm while oxygen supplies ran out and hypothermia set in. In all, eight lives were lost.

We men have suddenly found ourselves in a fierce storm as well.

In our advancement over the last thirty years to rightfully elevate and esteem women to a place of dignity, something unexpected has come upon us from those looking to exploit this consideration. While we've made great strides for the rights of our female counterparts, the pendulum has unexpectedly swung way over to the other side, with the result that true manhood is becoming almost endangered. Masculinity has been under attack and devalued to a point that now it is regarded as what's wrong in society! Men are often viewed as suspect unless they prove themselves harmless, leaving them inhibited and reluctant to step out and institute any type of spiritual leadership.

We all know that for years men have been made to look like bumbling fools on TV, their incompetence often corrected by women and children. A recent study done by a student from Brigham Young University showed that every 3.24 minutes on popular Disney shows for Tweens involving families, a dad "acts like a buffoon." And 50 percent of children watching "Daddy the dummy" reacted negatively by rolling their eyes, making a critical remark about him, acting annoyed, or walking away from the screen when the father spoke. What was once regarded as a harmless jest is now what men are starting to believe about themselves.

On the big screen men are also often depicted as weak and frightened, in need of assistance; it's the new normal. Women, on the other hand, are frequently portrayed as the only true, strong, and compassionate leaders who can save the day. This role reversal is seen clearly in the tremendously successful movie franchises like the *Hunger Games, Divergent Series,* and recently rebooted *Star Wars* prequels.

News media outlets continually add fuel to the fire. When atrocities are committed by violent men, especially domestic violence, the details are blasted on repeat, highlighting men's depraved actions, yet little is reported when women are the perpetrators. NewsCast Media cites that "the mainstream media seems to imply that men are the sole perpetrators of violence against women, but research shows otherwise." Violence is emphasized as it occurs *to* women and minimized when men are the victims of violent acts. The message: men are the reason for the evil in this world!

In the public educational system it's no secret boys are punished in school for acting more aggressively, which is their nature. Boys are made to sit quietly and learn as girls. When they do not comply or "behave," parents are urged to medicate them. This anti-boy approach, set in motion at the primary school level, is causing them to fall behind and avoid education as more women now graduate from college and go on to graduate school than men. According to the latest released White House Council of Economic Advisers report, women are increasingly becoming more educated than men.

The world has set in motion a reprogramming to redefine manhood: men are generally seen as problematic, oppressive, and needing to act more like women. And many are buying into this evaluation. More and more guys are prone to act passively in order to be accepted in society. Even Christian men are concerned with proving they are harmless and unoffensive, which is troublesome!

Instead of focusing on promoting truth and the gospel, which may at times be seen as confrontational, men think it's better to just keep quiet and go about their business than to cause conflict by objecting to the ways of the world. That's not good. And it all stems from an attack on manhood in our society.

In order to be a Christian in our world, one has to be strong and bold and exhibit manlike traits at times. Paul told the church at Corinth, "Be watchful, stand firm in the faith, act like men, be strong" (1 Cor. 16:13, ESV). Yet actually we're asleep in our manhood from being shamed and pushed down. That's the reality. It's time to wake up. The rooster is crowing. Manliness and masculinity are attributes to be desired. It's a good thing to be male! (I can't believe I even have to say that!) God made masculinity just as he made femininity to represent him. "God created human beings in his own image. In the image of God he created them; male and female he created them" (Gen. 1:27, ESV).

Interestingly, right after God declares the overarching purpose for mankind to bear his image, he described how it will would be done: through masculinity and femininity, with masculine souls and feminine souls. Through the roles of manhood and womanhood God is declared in our world. And God is only glorified only when we live according to our roles. God's not looking for gender neutrality; if he were, he wouldn't have made the differences.

Women are beautiful, amazing, and wonderful. I don't even need to state it, but I will. Most of us would not have a sense of purpose without them. Listen to a country music radio station for a while, and you'll see what most of the guys are enamored with and continually sing about—women! I'd be lost without the woman in my life, and our world would have a lot less beauty and grace. But we must be reminded that God needs men, too; we're invaluable for many reasons. And he especially uses man's bold initiative, strength, and daring spirit to spiritually lead and further his kingdom in a world where there is fierce opposition against it.

God came into this world as a man and chose twelve men to continue his mission. Women, of course, are just as important in furthering the kingdom but in their unique way. What's lacking now, what we need at the present time, is to esteem men in a world where they are no longer sense their value. They are extremely prized and vitally important to God, as Pastor Kenny Luck unabashedly states in *Sleeping Giant*: "Without men there can be no movement of God."

Why do society and the world devalue men? It's the work of Satan. It is such the work of the enemy to be so subtle and crafty in this way. If the devil can take men out, make them feel condemned—especially good men— then the witness and the ways of God will be greatly suppressed! Author John Eldredge states it correctly when he says in *Wild at Heart*, "The devil fears you and me because a good man thwarts his purposes."

Men have the ability to set the tone for good in our world or for evil. We can lead and influence others to live for the glory of God or unto destruction. It is true, men have often abused their positions of influence and headship for selfish and evil purposes; this is one of the reasons they are devalued in society today, (almost all acts of terror are committed by men). But the call is going out now to renew ourselves unto good and God's purposes: "With good men in authority, the people rejoice" (Prov. 29:2, TLB). We're not using the available resource God has given to bring blessing in our world: men!

Men are very important for the establishment of peace and order in our world. Instead of looking at men and boys as potential problems, we need to see them again as budding initiators for establishing goodness and justice.

Why should men be regarded with such weight of influence? Why do they have that position? God made it that way—he did it! It's the created order. God created man first, as we see in Genesis 2, and that means something. He could have created man and woman simultaneously but didn't for a reason, and this communicates an important message. The apostle Paul stated plainly: "I want you to understand this: The head of every man is Christ, the head of a woman is the man, and the head of Christ is God" (1 Cor. 11:3, NCV).

Women don't have any less value or worth than men because they're not the head, just as Christ isn't any less than God. It's just the order God has set in place in our world. It will not be so in heaven (see Matt 22:30). The apostle Paul explained that now men and women have different roles and responsibilities in glorifying God: "Man ought not to cover his head, since he is the image and glory of God, but woman is the glory of man" (1 Cor. 11:7, ESV). Does this mean women don't glorify God? Of course not—of course they do! But she also is to glorify God through her supportive role in glorifying the man.

Women have a dual focus both on their husbands and on God. The words *glory* and *glorify* mean to represent or declare the essence and character of another. It is a woman's primary responsibility as a wife to come along side and promote her man and support his leadership as unto the Lord. In doing so she declares God's glory, just like as Christ did for the Father. That is why down through the ages women usually took men's last names, (yet for the last thirty years this tradition is being observed less and less) and why it's so important to have our daughters marry Christian men!

According to scripture, men hold an important place in that they glorify and represent God alone through Christ. Men do not also represent women. Their purpose is to solely declare and show forth the virtues of God in the way they live, influencing their families to follow their lead. They're to represent God in his authority, his love, his truth, his kindness, his patience, justice, and a whole lot more, which will have a major effect on the rest of the family and community.

Not surprisingly, then, if men aren't seeking God in their lives, they won't see favorable results with their children. One study in Europe showed if a father goes irregularly to church regardless of what the mother does, between half and two-thirds of their offspring will find themselves coming to the church later, regularly or semi-regularly. But if a father does not go to church, no matter how devout the mother is, only one child in fifty will become a regular worshipper.

The bottom line is, if we men don't change our hearts, the impact on our families, churches, and world is devastating! I hope you're starting to see the importance we have. This is one of the reasons why celebrating manhood and masculinity should be a priority of ministry in all churches.

It is said a man's greatest need is significance. And many men lose their way because they don't have a sense that their lives matter. They don't believe they have any value. The National Center for Health Statistics released a study in 2016 showing depression in men has been on the rise for some time, with the suicide rate escalating to a rate of 3.5 times higher than that of women. But the reason so many men are in a fog today is that they're letting the world rather than God define their worth. Understanding God's purpose for man will begin to rub off the heavy tarnish the world has been putting on our identity. Underneath is something very valuable.

Man's significance or worth truly comes from who he is in relation to God. He's not made to exist as an entity unto himself! He exists for God and God's purposes. Stephen Mansfield's *Book of Manly Men* righty states, "Manly men live to the glory of God. . . . He cannot fulfill his role without doing so for the glory of God." What you and I are looking for to satisfy our manly souls out in the world, we will only find by living for God's glory.

This brings us to the A in ARISE. The first thing we need to get back on track and rise up as God's spiritual leaders is to be *after God's heart and glory*. A spiritual leader seeks after God. Make that your overarching grand pursuit again. All great spiritual leaders do! That's really why we're here, to seek and know God.

The psalmist wrote, "My soul thirsts for God, for the living God. When shall I come and appear before God?" (Ps. 42:2, ESV) Moses desired the same as he cried out, "Please show me your glory" (Exod. 33:18, ESV). Spiritual leaders continuously seek after God and desire to get close to him, the prophet Jeremiah tells us how, "You will seek me and find me when you seek me with all your heart" (Jer. 29:13, NIV).

Where does your mind go when you're alone? Instead of always thinking about the job, the next game, what's needed on the house, or where would be cool to go for vacation, try to think some about God's things, such as, *What are his plans and purposes in this world and for me personally?*

If you have no desire to think this way, pray and ask God to help you "set your mind on things above" (Col. 3:2, NASB), to have a hunger for him. Ask him to show you what's blocking you from seeking and thinking about him. He will reveal it! Something else must be more important to you. Spiritual leaders are conscious of God and have him on their minds. You can't live for the glory of God unless you do so.

As men we need to reclaim the truth of who we are. We're extremely valuable to lead in promoting God's purposes and represent him in this world. In fact, we won't find the true expression of manhood without seeking *after* God and living to glorify him.

So how do you really live for the glory of God? Is it speaking in King James English and living a rigid and restrictive life? No, it's something a lot more dynamic and exciting! Let's see how.

A tree gives glory to God in being a tree.
For in being what it means to be it is obeying God.

Thomas Merton

So whether you eat or drink or whatever you do,
do it all for the glory of God.

St. Paul (1 Cor. 10:31)

We weren't meant to be somebody,
we were meant to know somebody.

John Piper

CHAPTER 3

DAYBREAK

There's a true story that took place almost a hundred years ago that bears repeating—especially for the younger guys who probably don't know about it and for those of us who may have forgotten. This story, which inspired the film *Chariots of Fire*, showcases a man who exemplified seeking *after God's heart and glory,* the first principle we've discovered in ARISE.

Back in the 1920s a Scottish athlete by the name of Eric Liddell, who was a devout Christian, rose to prominence for his speed and abilities on the track, winning many events in the United Kingdom with his unorthodox style of running. While attending Edinburgh University to prepare for the mission field in China, he also trained for 1924 Olympic Games.

As the games approached he found out the 100 meter races, his best event, was scheduled for Sunday. This seriously troubled him. For he was convicted that he shouldn't compete or play sports on the Lord's Day, and he had encouraged others not to do so, especially younger lads who looked up to him. To run would be to compromise his principles and be hypocritical. So he switched to the 400 meter with just a few months to go before the games, a decision both the British parliament and the press criticized as reported in *the Guardian*.

★★★

Arriving in Paris, Sunday came and Liddell preached at a nearby church while the 100 meter heats took place in the stadium won easily by his rival, Harold Abrams.

Later that week when the 400 final event came all eyes were on him. At the starting line the US Olympic masseur slipped a piece of paper into his hand with 1 Samuel 2:30 written on it: "Those who honor me I will honor." Even with the worst lane position, lane 6, he pulled away from the pack and ran with all his might. The flying Scotsman finished 6 yards ahead of his nearest rival as God rewarded him the gold metal as he smashed the world record. The stadium went into a frenzy, the sports world was blown away, and Christians rejoiced.

That's living for the glory of God! Eric Liddell put honoring God above his own ambitions and his own glory. Besides the conviction that Sunday should be treated differently, with no indulging in sports, he believed that to say and live one way your whole life, then suddenly change due to certain circumstances would be hypocritical, show lack of character, and degrade God's name.

Now a lot of good Christian athletes rightly believe in God's grace and freedom in Christ to play sports on Sunday, so how about an example of living for God's glory a little closer to home? Maybe you've run into some hard times in your marriage and the woman you work with at the office is looking quite fine, and you feel an attraction there. Do you begin to leave your wife and pursue the coworker, or do you stay and work on your relationship with your wife, knowing God is faithful and you need to be faithful also?

Integrity is to live out what you believe to be right and wrong based on how God is and what honors him, even unto your own hurt. This quality is virtually nonexistent in our society today. It's not something considered valuable or sought after much anymore, yet we men must recapture it again. When we do, we'll begin to sense our importance and value again.

It's our job to reset these foundations of living for the glory of God, which takes courage, faith, and sacrifice at times. But God notices, and "He is a rewarder of those who seek him" (Heb. 11:6, NASB).

But let's back up for a second. If we're supposed to be living for God's glory, we need a better idea of what the glory of God is! Just what exactly is it? Automatically some of us think of it as some sort of bright light. The glory of God shone on the shepherds watching their flocks when the angels came and announced the birth of Jesus. And without a doubt actual light comes from the throne of God. At one time Jesus took a few of his closest disciples up on a mountain to reveal who he truly was; for a moment he unveiled himself, and bright light shone from his entire being. But the light represents something. The glory of God is not just light—it is the extreme excellence of his virtues and character. It's the wonderful qualities of his person, the manifestation of who he is, his nature and attributes that are so much purer than and superior to mankind's. Things like uniqueness, righteousness, faithfulness, power, beauty, goodness, grace, justice, love, mercy, faithfulness, and wisdom are just a few. John Piper says, "The glory of God is the infinite beauty and greatness of God's manifold perfections." W. E. Vine in his dictionary defines it as "the nature and acts of God in self manifestation." It's the revealing of who he is by what he does!

God has marvelously been revealing himself more and more since the beginning of time! The fancy theological term is *progressive revelation,* with the final revelation of his glory being the coming of Jesus. That's where we see the heart of God in fullness. Jesus is "the flawless expression of the nature of God" (Heb. 1:3, PHILLIPS).

The glory of God has reached its fullest expression in Jesus. That's why he said, "I am the light of the world" (John 8:12, ESV). The deepest revelation of God is in the person of Jesus. His mercy, love, grace, goodness, kindness, power, wisdom, and so much more have now been made known through the coming of Jesus and the gospel. That's why the apostle John could say referring to Jesus,

"The darkness is passing away and the true light is already shining" (1 John 2:8, ESV).

By understanding and believing in the work and person of Jesus, we begin to take in the glory of God! "For God, who said, 'Let there be light in the darkness,' has made this light shine in our hearts so we could know the glory of God that is seen in the face of Jesus Christ" (2 Cor. 4:6, NLT).

You see, before Jesus came, in Old Testament times God had only partially revealed himself. God's people saw his power and justice and his holiness and love, but in a very limited way. God even told his people Israel, *You really don't know me yet* by giving them an outward visual. What was that visual? It was the tabernacle, which later became the temple. In that temple the priests could only go to the first compartment, or room called *the holy place,* to present sacrifices to God. But once a year the high priest was allowed to enter into the inner room, where the ark of the covenant stood, and God's glory shone. This symbolized the fact that the way to get close to God and really know him wasn't possible yet. A heavy curtain separated this inner sanctuary from the outer where the priests were allowed on a daily basis. As the writer of Hebrews records, "Only the high priest ever entered the Most Holy Place, and only once a year. By these regulations the Holy Spirit revealed that the entrance to the Most Holy Place was not freely open as long as the Tabernacle and the system it represented were still in use" (Heb. 9:7–8, NLT).

Interestingly, what happened when Jesus died? That curtain was literally torn in two (see Matt. 27:51).

In response to Jesus' final sacrifice, God said in essence, *"You're forgiven! You don't have to fall short of my glory and be kept from me anymore* [see Rom. 3:23]. *You can come near now and start to get a much more clearer understanding of me, know my glory, and reflect my character yourselves."* That's what Jesus did. What was lost through the fall—kept from the glory of God and deeply knowing him—he regained for us.

Just as we can't look directly into the sun, we will never be able to *fully* grasp who God is and his glory known through Jesus, even with all eternity before us. But oh, it shines! And seeing the glory of God with our heart and mind is like sunlight on a budding tree in springtime, like photosynthesis to a leaf: His light brings life and effervescence, joy and renewal to satisfy our thirsty soul. "And this is eternal life, that they know you, the only true God, and Jesus Christ whom you have sent" (John 17:3, ESV).

Now with this light of understanding, daybreak can happen in our life. We can reflect who God is, and begin to shine as image-bearers of him in the way we live. It's why Jesus said "You are the light of the world" (Matt. 5:14, NASB).

Jesus shows us how to perfectly live out that glory for others to see by his recorded life. That's why he said, "Follow me"! By following him and learning his ways we can reveal more and more glory of God for an ever-continuing flow of life and joy in our souls, while also making a powerful impact on our world. "I am the light of the world. Whoever follows me will not walk in darkness, but will have the light of life" (John 8:12, ESV).

Nothing compares to living for the glory of God! It's the meaning of life. And we men have to lead in it, not only to thwart evil but also to show others how they can partake of this amazing purpose-filled life and not wither away in their souls.

So let's rise and shine! We have the honor and privilege to declare who God is with our life; to live as God, each in our own unique way! Is there any better existence?! But how can we see his glory regularly? How can we begin to come into this intimate knowledge of him? We can't represent someone if we don't really know them! We'll see how we can with the R in ARISE.

A.R.I.S.E.

R—READ

But all of us who are Christians have no veils on our faces,
but reflect like mirrors the glory of the Lord

St. Paul (2 Cor 3:18)

You are a mirror of yourself in others. Whatever you want, give.
Be the best reflection of yourself.

Karen A. Baquiran

The man who would truly know God must give time to Him.

A. W. Tozer

CHAPTER 4

AVOIDING THE FUNHOUSE

It was a breezy, warm day in late spring and we were filled with excitement about entering our new home in Lancaster, Pennsylvania. Along with the buzzing of the bumblebees on the budding flowers was the buzz of anticipation in both my wife and me and among the small congregation that had just brought me on to be their senior pastor. After my time youth pastoring, I welcomed this position with joy. And I thought it would be a great idea to have a Help-the-Pastor-Move-In Day to unload the truck and to get to know folks.

And so on that Friday afternoon, many decided to lend a hand. We financed this move ourselves because the church did not have a budget for moving. So we rented the Penske truck, and my father-in-law provided boxes.

He was a bartender and cook at the local pub in his postretirement years, and we obtained a lot of good boxes from there; however, they were a certain type of boxes. And we didn't think anything of it. But we seriously underestimated the ultraconservative church culture we moving into. The look on the faces of those lovely Mennonite folk (some believed even coffee was a mind-altering drug) said it all. As they unloaded the truck full of Budweiser, Jack Daniel's, and Corona boxes, I knew what they were thinking: *Good night, what have we hired?!*

Being misunderstood is no fun. Singer Bruce Springsteen said his "Born in the USA" song (and album) was completely misunderstood. People believed it was an anthem to celebrate nationalism when it really was describing all he thought was wrong with the country. (He didn't seem to complain too loudly, though—I guess selling thirty million copies had something to do with it.) But being misunderstood causes a disconnect between parties, bringing frustration and preventing true fellowship and intimacy. It's only a matter of time before the parties separate from each other. I say that from experience—the pastorate I just mentioned didn't last too long. I've also seen that with marriages resulting in divorce. Conversely it's an act of love and trust to sincerely want to understand someone and know his or her heart.

God is often misunderstood. I don't need to mention the atrocities that go on in the world in the name of God (or *Allah,* which means "the god" in Arab): shootings, murders, bombings, sexual sins. Or how about in Western civilization where God is what you want him or her to be? Make up your own version of God, and worship it according to your desires, whether your lifestyle is self-indulgent or highly restrictive. If it works for you, more power to you!

Oh, the patience of God. How we cringe and passionately object when we are misrepresented and misunderstood by someone. How must God feel?

In order to live for God's glory and be a spiritual leader, we want be a true reflection of who God is, not like a mirror in a funhouse that distorts a person. So we have to seek to know him in truth. Think about it: If you want to know somebody and get close and friendly, you have to communicate with them. Find out what they like. Ask questions and listen. It's the same with God.

And we have the resource we need to do so: God's Word. The Bible, which brings us to the R in ARISE: *read* and study the scriptures.

First and foremost, we need the Word the way we need food. We'll wither spiritually without it! If we only knew what a precious commodity sits on the shelf: The very words of God to give us life and hope, wisdom and strength, to radically transform lives! Yet many of us just run right out the door each day leaving it to collect dust. You know, it only takes about ten minutes to read a little something and another five to pray—that's a good start.

Maybe you're one of those exercise guys who runs, swims, or cycles. Such people are often militant about their regimen. Can't miss it or the day is ruined. Rain or shine, eighty-five degrees or thirty-five, they're out there! That's great for the mind and body, but what about the spirit and soul? What about the heart? We need to apply that same commitment to how we approach feeding on and digging into the Word of God.

The Word itself speaks of this: "Like newborn infants, long for the pure spiritual milk, that by it you may grow up into salvation" (1 Pet. 2:2, ESV). "Man does not live by bread alone, but man lives by every word that comes from the mouth of the LORD" (Deut. 8:3, ESV).

Before we accepted the truth of Jesus, received his Spirit, and became reconciled to God, we operated according to our souls. Our feelings, intellects, or wills drove us. If it felt good, was logical, or really desired—we did it! And many of us have operated according to this method and have created a disastrous mess in our lives and in the lives of those we influence.

But now as believers in Christ we are to let our minds, wills, and emotions be controlled by our spirit, the deepest part of us and where the Holy Spirit dwells. We are to have, as Watchman Nee stated in his *Spiritual Man,* "a spirit-controlled soul." Paul wrote, "Walk by the Spirit, and you will not gratify the desires of the flesh" (Gal. 5:16, ESV). We don't act on impulse or merely by reason or feelings anymore; we look to be guided by the Spirit. And we need to grow and strengthen that habit by feeding on the truth of the scriptures.

The classic story in Scripture emphasizing the need to feed on the Word to get strong is seen in Exodus 16. When the children of Israel wandered in the desert for forty years, each morning, before the sun got hot, they gathered bread that had fallen from heaven the night before. They couldn't gather a lot and store it for multiple days—it rotted overnight. They could collect only what they would eat that day. Clearly this is a literal example of what we are to do daily with the Scriptures. In John 6 Jesus declared himself the Bread that came down from heaven and instructed us to feed on the understanding of him: "The words I have spoken to you are spirit and they are life" (John 6:63, NIV).

Someone said reading and studying the Word is like making a cup of tea. The longer you leave the tea bag in the water to steep, the stronger the tea. The length of time we spend with the Word of God determines how much we absorb it, and the longer we do so, the stronger we become!

We will shrivel spiritually and put our spirits in a coma if we don't consume spiritual food each day. Soon we'll be back to running on soul, looking to sedate our ache inside through vices like busyness, alcohol, drugs, porn, sex, food, exercise, gaming, or movies rather than feeding on Christ. The world runs on soul and seeks to influence us to do the same, which brings bondage and despair. By feeding our spirits and letting the Holy Spirit flow in our hearts, we can say *no* to the world and its pressures and begin to rid ourselves of what's causing us to be poor reflections of God's glory. Paul urged us, "Do not allow this world to mold you in its own image. Instead, be transformed from the inside out by renewing your mind. As a result, you will be able to discern what God wills and whatever God finds good, pleasing, and complete" (Rom. 12:2, VOICE).

It's through the scriptures, that our reflection of God gets bright. It's where we learn to "cast off the deeds of darkness and put on the armor of light" (Rom. 13:12,

NIV). The Word teaches us how to live holy, as God is. Jesus said right before he went to the cross in his high priestly prayer: "Make them holy by your truth; teach them your word, which is truth" (John 17:17, NTL).

But then we also need the Word to know how to refute the misconceptions and errors about God that are all around us. Knowing the truth of scripture is how we fight against the deception of the darkness; it is our weapon against it. "All Scripture is breathed out by God and profitable for teaching, for reproof, for correction, and for training in righteousness, that the man of God may be complete, equipped for every good work" (2 Tim. 3:16–17, ESV).

As mentioned, there is a lot of evil craziness and terror in this world because of a faulty view of who God is and what he wants! For example, adherents to the Islam religion believe Allah is quite rigid and demands people to live a certain way—and if they don't, he's angry and wants to destroy them. Therefore it's okay for the followers to act that judgment out. But they misunderstand the merciful, gracious, and patient God who says in the scriptures, "'I take no pleasure in the death of the wicked, but rather that they turn from their ways and live'" (Ezek. 33:11, NIV). And in the New Testament we read that God is "not wishing that any should perish, but that all should reach repentance" (2 Pet. 3:9, ESV).

God doesn't want to destroy us! He wants all to come into his forgiveness and experience his mercy and grace. He said this plainly though the prophet: "I desire mercy, not sacrifice, and acknowledgment of God rather than burnt offerings" (Hosea 6:6, NIV).

By knowing the Word of God we can combat wrong thinking immediately and not let it spread in our hearts or in others. Until we get some scriptural knowledge, God can't really use us to fight against darkness. We won't know what's good and what's bad in his sight and be able to refute erroneous teaching. As roosters, you and I can't declare the light has come, help open people's eyes, and be good guides to God unless we know the truth and are growing in the knowledge of Christ! Hosea wrote, "My people are destroyed for lack of knowledge" (Hosea 4:6, ESV). Paul also emphasized this point: "No longer walk as the Gentiles do, in the futility of their minds. They are darkened in their understanding, alienated from the life of God because of the ignorance that is in them, due to their hardness of heart" (Eph. 4:17–18, ESV).

Let's be reminded again that we're in a serious battle against the powers of darkness and evil to control hearts and minds, to keep them from the truth. Having the Word in us is the only way we advance the kingdom of God and lead people out from being Satan's captives in darkness and bondage into the marvelous light and incredible joy Jesus offers. "And you will know the truth, and the truth shall set you free" (John 8:32, ESV). Truth that sets us free comes from the Word. You have to have the Word!

And if you think about it, how did Jesus rescue us from the grasp of Satan and the stronghold of serving sin? He died on the cross, but also through his teaching. If he didn't speak the word of the gospel along with that act, we wouldn't know what God's true heart is toward us and understand the salvation his death on that cross brings. The writer of Hebrews confirms, "How shall we escape if we refuse to pay proper attention to the salvation that is offered us today? For this salvation came first through the words of the Lord himself: it was confirmed for our hearing by men who had heard him speak" (Heb. 2:3, PHILLIPS).

Jesus came from heaven and spoke the Word of God to declare who God is, and what he's done for us (John 17:8). He's referred to as the Word of God . . . the expression of God. "The Word became a human being and lived here with us" (John 1:14, CEV). Gabelien states in his time-honored *Annotated Bible*, "As the invisible thought is expressed by the corresponding Word, He is the revealer of the mind and will of God."

Jesus' primary goal before he died was to communicate the truth of God. And we as his followers must seek to do the same. If the business of Jesus was to declare who God is, his plan and salvation, as little Christs (which is what *Christian* means), our business should be the same. To do so we must make knowing the Word a priority.

Perhaps you're thinking, "I just don't have the time with the heavy demands on my job and family pressures to study the word." I've been there. But here's the promise you can take to take to the bank: "Seek first the kingdom of God and his righteousness, and all these things will be added to you" (Matt. 6:33, ESV).

When you devote time to seeking God and working on building his kingdom as a spiritual leader, he has a way of smoothing things out with extra help in our other responsibilities like family, work, friends, and fun. I've seen it happen in my own life often. It will happen in yours. Trust him.

Maybe you could make the time but you're just not that motivated yet. Let's see if we can build a hunger and interest for God's word in the next chapter.

A thorough knowledge of the Bible is worth more than a college education.

Theodore Roosevelt

I wish I had studied more and preached less.

Billy Graham

Visit many good books, but live in the Bible.

Charles Spurgeon

CHAPTER 5

BREAK THE FAST

There's a hilarious clip in the movie *How the Grinch Stole Christmas* (the one with Jim Carrey as the Grinch; see http://www.wingclips.com/movie-clips/how-the-grinch-stole-christmas/the-book-says). In it the mayor of Whoville announces to the town that it is time to nominate that year's Cheermeister, the one who leads the way in promoting good cheer and the celebration of Christmas. And from deep in the crowd a small girl's voice yells, "I nominate the Grinch!" In response the mayor pulls out *The Book of Who* and quotes a verse as to why the Grinch is a bad choice for Cheermeister. He's unaware that Cindy Lou knows her "scriptures of Who" and replies, "But *The Book of Who* says this, too: 'No matter how different a Who may appear, he will always be welcome with holiday cheer.'" The mayor becomes visibly flustered as he's outwitted and out-versed by the young girl, and he creates a phony verse that disqualifies the Grinch again. She replies, "You made that up! It doesn't say that. . . . What page?" She goes on to skillfully apply her knowledge of *The Book of Who* using the appropriate verses, both schooling and humiliating the mayor so he has to nominate the Grinch for Cheermeister. Epic!

That scene perfectly sums up how familiar we need to be with the scriptures. It is no new thing that people take a piece of scripture out of context, twist it, and use it for their own agendas and desires. The devil did it with Jesus when he tempted him (Matt. 4).

As roosters leading the way to the presence of God, we must know how to get there. It requires spiritual wisdom and knowledge to avoid the wrong paths. That comes only from the study of scripture.

Paul wrote to Timothy, "Do your best to present yourself to God as one approved, a workman who does not need to be ashamed and who correctly handles the word of truth" (2 Tim. 2:15, NIV). But just like the mayor of Whoville, too many have neglected this habit and maintain only a shallow understanding of the general truths of scripture rather than pursuing an accurate, in-depth knowledge. I know too many guys that have been living on the *Daily Bread* diet for far too long. Devotionals are great short meditations, but if you have been a Christian for years and that's your only personal intake of the Bible, I can guarantee you're failing to become a leader.

In refusing to deepen your understanding of the scriptures you're staying a spiritual adolescent, while God wants us to grow "until we all attain to the unity of the faith and of the knowledge of the Son of God, to mature manhood, to the measure of the stature of the fullness of Christ" (Eph. 4:13, ESV). It's time to take it up a serious notch or two. Make studying the Word of God top priority in your life. Don't leave it to the "experts" or theologians to pursue. Jesus wants all of us to be experts in understanding his truth and accurately handling the scriptures.

Now you might honestly say, "I just can't! I'm bored to tears trying, and it doesn't accomplish anything!" Let's take a look and see what we can do to acquire more of a hunger for the Word, and "break the fast" of the study of scripture.

It begins with our approach to the Bible, our view of it. Do we really believe it's God's Word? That's a critical presupposition and foundation for devoting yourself to its study. You have to believe it's the inerrant (without error, no untruths, incapable of being wrong) message from the all-powerful Creator of the universe, or you will have no serious drive to treasure and study it.

Ken Berding, professor at Biola University, says Bible knowledge is at an all-time low, in fact at a crisis point, and a contributing factor is the way we view it. In his *Biola* magazine article "Crisis of Biblical Illiteracy and What We Can Do about It" he states,

★★★

Many Americans don't consider the Bible to be authoritative, that is they don't consider the Bible to "place a claim on their lives." Oh, it's important in a general sort of way . . . but it's a far cry [from] believing God has communicated His Will through this book and [it is] binding on your actions. Only one third believe the Bible is the inerrant Word of God. Some of this is because they have breathed in Post Modernism and distrust a meta narrative—an overarching grand truth of purpose and goals. Americans don't consider the Bible to be authoritative."

★★★

This is our culture: The devil is constantly attacking the credibility of scripture. Unless you believe scripture contains the words of God, not only will you fail to highly value it, you'll lack power in your life to bring about change and blessing. Paul wrote, "We also constantly thank God that when you received the word of God which you heard from us, you accepted it not as the word of men, but for what it really is, the word of God, which also performs its work in you who believe" (1 Thess. 2:13, NASB).

Bible.org is a website offering many resources, including articles on our faith and the status of the Bible. I'll quote from it here showing just how special the Bible is, like no other book:

★★★

The Bible was written over a period of 1600 years by a wide diversity of over 40 authors from many different locations, and under a wide variety of [ways transmitted]. The Bible is not one book but a collection of 66 books whose authors came from all walks of life. Some kings, some peasants, philosophers, fishermen, physicians, statesmen, poets, and farmers. They lived in a variety of cultures at different times and are different in their make-up. Yet, regardless of this diversity, it is bound together by perfect historical sequence. The books roll out perfectly over time, each connecting to the meet with unearning progression. Most importantly, in it is the anticipation, presentation, realization and exaltation of the most perfect person who ever walked the earth and whose glories are manifest in heaven.

★★★

The Bible is a miracle. From Genesis to Revelation it's about Jesus and God's plan around him. It's perfectly unified, without contradictions or inconsistencies: Only God by his Holy Spirit could've done that. He inspired each man to write it! All the other books that claim to be God's Word—*The Koran, The Book of Mormon,* portions of *Vedas* from Hinduism—were all written by people who say they had revelations from God. Each book was the result of one man's interpretation of "revelations" he claimed to see over one period of time, and you have to take his word; or you can read sixty-six books from forty different authors in different time periods in a volume that is completely unified in message. You can't even compare it to other "scriptures"! The Bible is not on the same level. It is certainly is the inerrant Word of God.

What are we doing about it? Can we really be bored by reading the Bible if we understand what it truly is?

The second reason we lose our appetite for the words of God is that we don't do what it says. "Don't I beg you, only hear the message, but put it into practice; otherwise you are merely deluding yourselves" (Jas. 1:22, PHILLIPS). The Bible is not like any other book. God's Word is powerful and causes a reaction. Either you respond to it and live out what it says, or you resist and ignore it. When you practice ignoring and resisting it, God doesn't give you more of his revelation. Not if it's just to be discarded again—he's too high and holy! He's a good steward of the riches of grace and revelation. He doesn't want to waste them on those who don't follow what it says.

If you're just reading for information and ignoring the instruction, he won't give you the good stuff, the *revelation* of his Word. It won't come alive but seem boring to you. The psalmist said, "Open my eyes, that I may see wondrous things from Your law" (Ps. 119:18, NKJV). It's the revealed Word of God that causes illumination, jubilation, and transformation. These qualities come from being doers of the Word.

In my song "Back on Track" from the record *Meta Me Nova,* I say, "Let your life show the truth that you already know, then more light will come." God has arranged that the only way we get more of the life-giving knowledge of him is if we seek to live like Christ, implement what we come to know. Paul wrote, "And so, from the day we heard, we have not ceased to pray for you, asking that you may be filled with the knowledge of his will in all spiritual wisdom and understanding, so as to walk in a manner worthy of the Lord, fully pleasing to him: bearing fruit in every good work and increasing in the knowledge of God" (Col. 1:9–10, ESV).

Let what you read impact the way you think and live. A lot of us don't want to adjust our lives, but we must be convinced that in applying the instruction of the Word of God we will come into a place of abundant blessing. "Blessed are those who keep my ways" (Prov. 8:32, NIV).

The third reason we have no desire for God's Word is that we consider other things more important. It's just not relevant or that valuable for everyday life and the things you're after. But the truth is, whatever we believe is more important than knowing God is an idol. Idols cause blindness, making it difficult to see or desire any spiritual truths in scripture—Paul described this principle in nonbelievers: "In their case the god of this world has blinded the minds of the unbelievers, to keep them from seeing the light of the gospel of the glory of Christ, who is the image of God" (2 Cor. 4:4, ESV). The light of understanding in believers can also get quite dim, causing blindness to spiritual truths and making them seem unimportant when we erect other "gods" in our heart above the Lord.

It's time for a little self-examination. What things are most important to you? What do you see and understand to be good and desirable? Why? Money and wealth are often a big one. It was in Jesus' time as well, as he said:

★★★

"But store up for yourselves treasures in heaven, where neither moth nor rust destroys, and where thieves do not break in and steal; for where your treasure is, there your heart [your wishes, your desires; that on which your life centers] will be also.

"The eye is the lamp of the body; so if your eye is clear [spiritually perceptive], your whole body will be full of light [benefiting from God's precepts]." (Matt. 6:20–22, AMP)

★★★

The things of this world are temporary. The apostle Paul wrote, "What is seen is temporary, what is unseen is eternal" (2 Cor. 4:18, NIV). We've got to start thinking and preparing for eternity—this life is fading fast! As country artist Kenny Chesney sings, "Don't blink—a hundred years goes faster than you think." Spiritual leaders have their eyes and hope on the future and what's coming. Ask God to do a work in you so you will truly want him more than anything, and to reveal what you worship and desire above him. That's a prayer he'll answer and once you knock off whatever it is on the throne of your heart, you'll start to see spiritually again.

Also make an effort to stop eating spiritual "junk food" so you're hungry for God's Word. Just as your mother told you not to spoil your supper when you came home from school, save your appetite for the most nourishing substance. Seek God through the Word, not your vice, whatever it is. Use that empty feeling we as fallen humans often get, to drive you to the scriptures to be filled with his Spirit, and at peace. Try not to always sedate yourself with the computer, social media, TV, smoking, drink, food, or whatever.

As you start or restart reading the Word in order to reflect the Lord, here are just a few very practical tips.

Always ask God to give you the desire for his Word to reveal truths to you: "Let me see clearly so that I may take in the amazing things coming from your law." (Ps. 119:18, VOICE). Read Psalm 119 every now and then. It's an inspiring exaltation of God's Word.

★★★

Get a good study Bible. Find a word-for-word translation like the New American Standard Bible, the English Standard Version, the New King James Version, or the Amplified Bible, because sometimes deeper meanings are unintentionally paraphrased out in the newer translations. But then also have alongside a good thought-for-thought or paraphrase Bible, such as the New Living Translation, the New Century Version, or *The Message* for readability.

Rather than read as much as you can, quickly, take a portion—a certain section or half a chapter—and ruminate on it. In other words, meditate on and ponder it. The term *chew on the cud* represents the idea. If you've ever seen a cow eat, you know he chews till it's really ground up because hay is hard to digest.

Don't fly through the scriptures as if you're reading the news, but slowly think about them. It's necessary to slow down in order to hear from God. Go over the passage a couple times and see what verses stand out. Look up the corresponding references on verses that seem important or confusing to you. Other Bible scriptures will help you understand and give more insight. All scholars know scripture is the best interpretation of scripture! Reading related scriptures takes you deeper.

Get a good Bible dictionary so you can look up words that are unfamiliar. Also acquire a good commentary set or two, written by others who have studied the text that you can read after you've done your own reading. Don't go right to the commentary after you read—let the Spirit give you his own thoughts first, write them down in a notebook, and then go to the commentary. You can't go wrong with commentaries by John MacArthur or Warren Wiersbe, as well as the *Bible Knowledge Commentary* and *Expositor's Bible Commentary* on your shelf.

Instead of plowing straight through the Bible from Genesis to Revelation, I suggest what a wise old preacher taught me: read three New Testament books, then one Old Testament book. Why? Because the New Testament books are shorter and you'll keep moving. But also this way the new covenant of grace will always be strong in your heart, and you'll be able to read the Old Testament from the vantage point of the more complete revelation in the New Testament.

When you read the Word, *listen.* God speaks, so anticipate hearing from him on subjects like his plan in Christ, new things about Jesus, (God wants us to know all we have through Jesus), things to change in your character, and spiritual goals to seek. He'll also speak on issues concerning that day and guidance in personal matters. But don't get caught up in seeking *only* personal applications. Too many of us, when reading the scriptures, immediately ask, *How does this apply to me? What do I have to do?* Rather, first we should ask, *What is there to learn and know about God? Where is Jesus in this passage, and how does his finished work on the cross impact what this portion of scripture says?* Then ask, *How does it apply to me?* In doing so we cultivate a heart of worship and love for God in knowing what he's done in Christ, which empowers us to make any change needed and then to serve.

Jesus even showed us the importance of a Christ-centered approach to understanding the scriptures. After his resurrection, two disciples traveled on the road to Emmaus to the nearby town of Jerusalem, and Jesus joined them, but they didn't realize it (Luke 24). He kept them from recognizing him. He did this because, as Joseph Prince affirms in *Destined to Reign,* he wanted to show how people could "see" him for generations to come until he appears physically again. Luke 24:27 (NASB) declares that with the Old Testament scriptures Jesus "explained to them the things concerning Himself" and said to look for him in the scriptures. He took the time to do this before he ascended to heaven, to show us that is the key to understanding the Bible and giving us life: always looking for him, and the things we have in Christ throughout all the scriptures.

Finally, we need to stop approaching the Bible as a rulebook. Too many view it that way. Many guys think that believing in Jesus means that they have the ability to obey God's commands if they just try hard enough. Their focus is still on obeying a code of behavior and laws of God, so they read the Bible that way.

But that's the "pre-Jesus" way to God. The truth is our flesh naturally rebels against the laws of God, so we won't really want to read the Bible approaching it that way! Because of Jesus, we're now in a new spot with God, a new position with him; we've received a new deal. Under the new covenant, which is a relationship based on love and grace, we serve God now in "in newness of the Spirit and not in the oldness of the letter [of the law]" (Rom. 7:6, NASB). It's a different approach. Serving in the Spirit means the Holy Spirit is in us, delights in us, and wants to live loving God and others. That Spirit inside just needs to grow and become our guiding influence.

The way to get the Spirit strong and flowing in us is to hang out with Jesus. Get stoked on understanding who he is, "in whom are hidden all the treasures of wisdom and knowledge" (Col. 2:3, ESV). Get to know what you are and have now in him.

When we start thinking about Jesus and appreciating him, the Spirit is released and moves in our heart and wants to fulfill the desires of God! This is serving God in the Spirit, and why it's important to always be looking for Christ in the scriptures.

So hopefully now your spiritual stomach is beginning to growl, and interest for knowing God again through his Word has been aroused. But to stay hungry and consistently want to seek after the knowledge of him, the next letter in ARISE is crucial for spiritual leaders.

A.R.I.S.E.

I—INSTRUCT

Teach your children well.

Crosby, Stills & Nash

I have come to believe that a great teacher is a great artist.
Teaching might even be the greatest of the arts since the medium
is the human mind and spirit.

John Steinbeck

Peter do you love me?. . . . feed my sheep.

Jesus

CHAPTER 6

TIDBITTING: FEEDING THE ROOST

More men play the state lottery than women. Men are about 1.5 times more likely to play, according to Kasey Henricks and David G. Embrick in their book, *State Looteries.* As for winning, you know you have better odds of getting struck by lightning! But even more important, winning—what would seem to be the greatest day imaginable—has turned into a curse for many lottery winners. It's not all it's cracked up to be. Winners often are quoted saying that they wish they had never won. Relationships change and life is different—usually not for the better.

Most tragic was Billie Bob Harrell Jr., who won the Texas Lottery in the late nineties. His winnings were a staggering $31 million. But less than two years after the win, the toll on his marriage and financial stress overwhelmed him, and Harrell committed suicide. Before his death he was quoted as saying, "Winning the lottery is the worst thing that ever happened to me."

I worked with a guy selling mortgages back in New Jersey when I was first married. He used to play the lottery, and I once said to him, "You know, a lot of people are destroyed when they win the lottery." He turned, looked at me, and said with that New York accent, "Oh yeah? Ruin me! Please!"

There's nothing wrong with getting wealthy if God allows it, but it's better to acquire it slowly. And don't make that your god—the thing you live for.

> Yes, a person is a fool to store up earthly wealth but not have a rich relationship with God. (Luke 12:21, NLT)

> Though your riches increase, do not set your heart on them. (Psalm 62:10, NIV)

If you look at people's New Year's resolutions and life goals, making more cash is usually at the top of the list, especially for the Millennial generation. But these riches are temporary; rather, we should make true riches our highest goal in life: to know God through Christ. This is treasure that lasts forever. The effort put into the relationship of knowing God here is taken with us when we die and translates into glory that will never fade for all eternity. That's an investment with a guaranteed huge payoff! So make sure to keep the building of your spiritual portfolio with God top priority.

Because here's the kicker regarding finding God and his spiritual truth: It is dependent on us desiring it above everything else. We can't casually glance at the knowledge of God now and then and expect to come into his eternal secrets and rich wisdom. We have to make it number one in life. Isn't he worth it?!

> Search for [insight and understanding] as you would for silver; seek them like hidden treasures. Then you will understand what it means to fear the Lord, and you will gain knowledge of God. (Proverbs 2:4–5, NLT)

In the last chapter we looked at some hints at how to stay hungry for God and maintain a desire to know him. There's one more hint I believe is so important it gets its own section. I've experienced this to be the most critical element in the pursuit of God: We need to be sharing what we know and have come to understand, open our mouths, and tell others the truth and knowledge of God. *Instruction* is the third component in ARISE.

★★★

I—*instruct* and teach your family, find a place in the church to teach, and speak spiritual truth to those in your world. This is the gas that keeps you seeking to know and understand God. As men and spiritual leaders, it's our job to instruct those under our care and in our sphere of influence with the Word. And as we give and empty out our cup of knowledge and understanding, it makes us thirst to go back and get more! Try it—it works! It's hard to stay hungry for the Word when you just sit around and take in, take in, take in, and never give out. We have to read, think, and study with the expectation that we're gonna speak these truths to others. That's the key.

Teaching the truth about God is the occupation of all Christians, but especially men. We should be telling others how to get to God or how to get closer to God, which is what life is all about. It's in man's nature to want to lead, teach, and tell others how to do something. We like to give input to help others, to feel we're responsible for their progress. Men are inclined to want to give advice, counsel, and instruction.

It's probably why we hate to stop and ask for directions. But we have no problem telling people how to get somewhere when they ask! (By the way, did you know why the children of Israel wandered around in the desert for forty years? Because even in biblical times, men wouldn't ask for directions.)

But think about it: When our wives come to us wanting to talk and get relational because they're feeling a rift in the relationship, bothered by something we said or did, what do we do? Naturally we approach it with a fix-it mentality, right? We respond, "Here's what you need to do. . . ." But all they really want is some time and affection—to be heard and know they're appreciated. We laugh at that "typical guy response," and there are times we do need to sit down, shut up, and just listen! But what is certain is that men's instincts say to fix with given instruction. And that's a good thing when used appropriately; God created that in us for a reason.

The first place we need to concentrate on providing instruction is in the home with our families. It's top priority. Look at what scripture says: "Fathers, do not provoke your children to anger but bring them up in the discipline and instruction of the Lord" (Ephesians 6:4, ESV).

★★★

"Tidbitting" is a term to describe what a rooster does when he finds food for the hens and chicks. He picks up the tidbit of food he has found and drops it several times, while circling it and making a certain sound. This attracts the hen to the food.

Someone has truthfully said, "Men are qualified to get married if they can teach the Word of God to their families." Wow, that would cut down on the wedding business for sure! It's not the church's job, or the pastor's job, or Christian school's job to instruct and train families. They help, but it's the fathers' responsibility, supported closely by their wives. It's so important that we lead and actively participate in this instruction at home, even though mom is a big part as well. As a matter of fact, the home is the place where men qualify or disqualify themselves to become more prominent spiritual leaders with a bigger influence. Some guys want to do great things for God, but they ignore their families—and doing big things for God starts with our families!

There you'll develop patience and perseverance, tenderness and firmness, sacrifice and selflessness. And be careful: Your actions must line up with your words because your family will call you on it. That's why the scriptures describe the qualifications of an elder in a church this way: "He must manage his own family well, having children who respect and obey him. For if a man cannot manage his own household, how can he take care of God's church?" (1 Tim. 3:4–5, NLT).

So make it a habit to carve out some time each day, after dinner or at bedtime, to read the scriptures and have a little family Bible study. Read a Bible story and expound a bit on it. Choose something you've read and studied in your own study time and then pray together. Be as consistent as you can, at least on the weekdays. It ends up being a great time of blessing and sets the tone in the house with you as the leader. The earlier you can start leading and instructing in your children's lives, the better.

I started while my kids were pretty young. Of course there was some fussing! Now they're college kids and in their twenties, but when they're home and we're able to sit down for a meal together, I still give a little Word to them, and they appreciate it, actively listening and making a comment or two.

Don't just use the formal gathering to teach; make the most of impromptu opportunities that arise each day too. During the casual times be diligent to notice moments you can bring in God's teaching or mention something about the Lord. Deuteronomy 6:6–7 (ESV) says, "And these words that I command you today shall be on your heart. You shall teach them diligently to your children, and shall talk of them when you sit in your house, and when you walk by the way, and when you lie down, and when you rise." In other words, look for the moments in your conversations and interaction to work in truth or instruction. The Holy Spirit will prompt you as you seek to practice this habit. Boy, if each guy did this in his house, the nation would be changed!

And here's the kicker with this: As we open our mouths to instruct and correct our kids to live the way that pleases God, we're teaching them to allow God to speak into their lives later on when we are not around, for the rest of their lives. If we don't teach them to stop and go God's way when they're young, they'll have an extremely hard time doing that later in life, especially in times of trouble. Ultimately they'll miss out on peace and blessing in their lives. That's why Proverbs 23 says, "Don't fail to discipline your children. . . . Physical discipline may well save them from death" (vv. 13–14, NLT).

Yes, save them from the "death" of horrible circumstances due to bad choices; from becoming delinquents and maybe ending up in jail! But also your instruction and discipline can "save" them eternally by teaching them to accept correction and instruction from God. You will have taught them how to be humble and be teachable, and turn toward what's good even when you're not around.

Teaching your family doesn't mean just the kids. Scripture says to nourish and cherish your wife "as Christ loved the church" (Eph. 5:25, NLT). We're also to give out the Word to our wives—but we don't teach them in the same manner we teach our children.

For your wife is a coheir with you and your associate in instructing the kids. To her you want to bring helpful words of encouragement to build her up in Christ. Tell her about some of the treasures you've been finding in the scriptures when you're driving or out to dinner. And let her know often how important her teaching and spiritual guidance is to the kids.

Family is a very important place to learn how to give out the Word as God's guide. A good rooster finds food for the ones in his care. We also need to be "tidbitting" spiritually, continuously feeding our loved ones with the truth of scripture. Once you get it going at home, or if you don't have a family to teach, you'll want to press on and look for the next area in which to instruct others with the *riches* of his Word, the Church.

Neglect not the gift that is within thee.

St. Paul (1 Tim 4:14)

Don't just delegate tasks to the next generation.
If you delegate tasks, you create followers. Instead,
delegate authority to create leaders.

Craig Groeschel

You are to follow no man further than he follows Christ.

John Collins

CHAPTER 7

BE LED TO LEAD

I had to do it! I couldn't back down now—I had my best suit on. Something inside urged me forward. My mouth was dry, my palms were sweaty, and my heart was beating so loud and fast I thought for sure others could hear it.

No, I wasn't about to ask out that cute redhead from seventh-period English. . . . I was in church. In the middle of an open worship service where anybody could get up and offer a prayer, announce a song to sing, read some scripture, or speak. And I was about to give it my first try.

I had grown up in a church where one of our services was Spirit-led, where there was no preset program led by just one or two people. Instead, all had a chance to offer up a particular word of worship as they felt led.

For years I watched my father, grandfather, and others take part at this gathering. And now in my early teens they would often remark after this service, "I didn't hear from you, brother," encouraging me to take part and say something simple to praise the Lord or give thanks. And now the moment had come.

I found myself rising to my feet, holding onto the back of the pew in front of me. With a shaky voice I said, "Can we sing 'God Be Horrified,' number ninety-six?"

Every person turned toward me with a smile. My buddy Ronnie, who was sitting next to me, hit me on the leg, tried not to laugh, and whispered loudly, "Dude, you said 'horrified!'"

Gulp. "I mean 'God Be Glorified.'"

I sat down and wanted to crawl under the pew, but the congregation started singing, and it sounded extra loud for some reason. They probably wanted to make sure they encouraged me despite my error. Afterward many said how nice it was to have me say something and that they liked the song.

Even though I made that blunder, a couple weeks later I spoke up again, this time without messing up the song's title. A week or two after that Ronnie got up the nerve and gave out his first song. From there I progressed to reading a psalm and offering a comment, and by the time I was sixteen or seventeen I was praying publicly at services. I was nineteen, in my second year of college, when I was given a Sunday evening to preach! The next year the elders gave me the high school Sunday school class because they saw me developing. After college I was given the opportunity to lead many ministries as a volunteer, going on to become a youth pastor and eventually a pastor, leading to the current parachurch ministry I have today.

None of this would have happened if I hadn't received opportunity, encouragement, and nurturing from the church to develop as a leader. It kindled a fire in my heart that burst into flame.

This brings us to a very important aspect of the I in ARISE—the instruction of others. We've talked about *instructing* as the spiritual leader of your family. Once you've developed that role, it is so important to find a place in the church to speak the Word. You can teach at Sunday school to kids, adults, a youth group, a small group, one-on-one discipling, you name it. Find a place there where you have the responsibility to give out the Word.

You might be tempted to think: *If I'm teaching at home, isn't that enough?* No. As a spiritual leader you always want to be looking to grow and expand your sphere of influence in God's kingdom according to his leading. This will drive you to study the Word more and bring you closer to the Lord. Don't be afraid or feel you don't have the right to seek to increase your responsibility in helping guide others in the church. The Lord will use that desire to expand his kingdom in his time and way. Meanwhile, at whatever level learn to speak the Word of God competently with confidence and conviction, whether you're working with kids or adults: "If anyone speaks, let him speak as the oracles of God" (1 Pet. 4:11, NKJV). Soon you'll begin to sense more power coming from you in your instruction, and a closeness to the Lord knowing you are his servant.

I have found, having served at various churches, that this precious opportunity to develop into a spiritual leader is not something to take for granted. In that little church I grew up in, there was an expectation for me to grow, so I'd help govern the church someday. I felt valued and important, which made me pursue spiritual things all the more. Walk into many churches today and this way of thinking, this view of men, is not readily apparent and is often nonexistent. Of course men are encouraged to attend, grow in their personal relationship with the Lord, and be active as volunteers. But there's no clear path to advance in communicating the truths of God to others and participating in the ministry with a view to becoming a serious leader in a church, whether developing men to become part of the leadership at the present fellowship or to be encouraged and supported to launch a new work somewhere else. That's a problem, as it stunts the growth of men into spiritual leaders. And this has to do with the church government, its structure, and philosophy of ministry.

Everyone wants to know why the church attracts more women than men, with the recent gender gap reported by the Barna Group at 61 percent women to 39 percent men. Most men don't want to go somewhere regularly where they have to be passive and in a continual support role in order to belong. It's not in our makeup! And that's a good thing—don't condemn it in yourself or others. Men must be offered a sense of ownership in the church, to see that ultimately it is their job, or will be their job, for the ministry there along with the pastor. That was the intention of the apostles when they set up the churches in the first century. Men need to be given the freedom, chance, privilege, and responsibility to lead the church. They shouldn't be stifled and ashamed to desire this because it's only regulated to the professional. Men will feel much more needed and significant when they have this opportunity, and more apt to commit. Obviously one must grow into leadership and become qualified, as it takes a good amount of time, along with humility. But guys must see they have a realistic opportunity to work toward a tangible goal of leadership in the church, so they make that a major part of their lives and start acting like it. Yet often this opportunity is kept from them with harmful results.

When a church keeps pushing men away from growing into ministerial leadership, it has negative repercussions on the rest of life. If men feel there's no real vision to go with their spiritual leadership, they back off in pursuing it personally, with their families, and in their communities. It has a serious negative trickle-down effect.

Author and pastor Kenny Luck states it plainly in *Sleeping Giant:* "If a man doesn't find his place of significance in the church, he'll go out in the world to find it." And the truth is, most men are not inspired in the long term to realign their lives and their life purpose to collect the offering, setting up and breaking down chairs, driving the golf cart, helping park cars, or assisting with child care. It's not gonna happen.

The problem is men aren't finding significance in the church. If men aren't sensing any real leadership potential, left continually to do tasks that don't seem to have much importance, you won't find many dedicated to the fellowship.

Again I'm referring to the overall structure and approach of the church, which is vitally important to the development of spiritually strong men. Is it one where laymen are kept at bay and pushed down while pastors and elders create an order that elevates them above everybody else and kept that way? Is it run by social status and money where only those with favorable social standing or high incomes get opportunity to become leaders in the church?

If you're not in a church where you feel deeply valued and encouraged to develop as far as possible and sense an openness to all men desiring to develop into church leaders—move on and find one that does. You're being robbed!

Much life and glory await you by growing into leadership, eldership, and co-governing the church. Don't let anyone block you, whether you are formally educated or not. There's got to be an understanding that each man has the privilege and responsibility to progress there. This should be the prevailing spirit. God made Peters (fishermen), and God made Pauls (scholars), and he uses them both as leaders to promote his kingdom.

Even with men who don't seek to hold an official leadership role in the local church, they should be expected to pursue a spiritual maturity level equal to it and then be honored as one. This will help keep the spiritual bar raised high for all men to follow after.

Men get strong when they are given spiritual leadership responsibility in the church, and it helps them to then be spiritually strong in the world. I'm convinced this lack of focus on male leadership in the church is causing our weak spiritual state in the nation and our communities to crumble.

Simply put, we can no longer leave the worship, instruction, and spiritual leadership to the pastor or "paid professional." That's not in the mind of Christ for his church. All men should be encouraged to develop, teach, learn to discern bad doctrine, and ultimately become co-leaders, whether visible or behind the scenes, to help give direction and guidance to the church.

By the amazing work of Jesus Christ who came, died, and rose again, we now all have the privilege and responsibilities the priests of the Old Testament had. No longer is spiritual leadership restricted to just a select few, as was the case in ancient Israel, the scene for our opening drama at the beginning of this book. Peter exclaims, "You are a chosen race, a royal priesthood, a holy nation, a people for his own possession, that you may proclaim the excellencies of Him who has called you out of darkness into His marvelous light" (1 Pet. 2:9, NASB). And John wrote in the last book of the Bible, "He has made us a Kingdom of priests for God his Father" (Rev. 1:6, NLT).

Because of Jesus, we have a new order in place. We are all priests, just as Martin Luther declared: "Every Christian is a cleric." Advantage and privilege are given to all, and men especially must step up and express their priesthood in the church. It glorifies Christ and his powerful work, bringing him worship when we do. Priests taught God's Word and ways to the people of Israel as well as ran the temple and offered up sacrifices. And men especially need to lead in doing so today in the church!

Who is keeping men down? I'm sorry to say that pastors can be those that inhibit men from growing into true spiritual leaders. They are seen as the spiritual specialist and looked to solely for shepherding, and many are glad to keep it that way.

But it's also the mentality of the saints and congregation that hold men down. Often church government is understood to run the same way a typical business corporation is, like Apple, AT&T, or Chevrolet. We assume the best plan is top-down management with the pastor as the CEO. It's efficient, orderly, and gets things done. But there's a huge difference between a regular business and the church. We're supposed to be looking out for our brother and helping them excel in leadership too.

The church is a *spiritual* organism, where Jesus is the head. " And he is the head of the body, the church" (Col. 1:18, ESV). His ways are higher than our ways, so his priorities and what determines progress look different from ours. We should be looking for what God seeks: true growth, especially among men, which will have an effect on all.

Pastors and teachers are indeed necessary. But instead of seeking to distance themselves above others, which can naturally creep in due to many current church structures, they should encourage and develop faithful, qualified men to come alongside them and share the responsibility.

Biblically, a pastor is one of the elders, no higher. And the burden of caring for, ministering, and overseeing the flock, is to be done by a plurality of elders.

How a church views men will have an effect on their spiritual growth. We can't ignore men and God's *intended* church government that promotes every man as a potential and expected spiritual leader there. When this structure is place, *then* we'll see attendance of men in church increase, and an impact on society.

In the New Testament, the apostle Paul actually set up churches to run by themselves, and Jesus came to work himself out of a job! You can see this vividly in the story of the feeding of the five thousand. In Matthew 14, Jesus went away to be alone for a while. But the crowds found out and like paparazzi made their way to catch up with him. And unlike an annoyed pop star seeking privacy, Jesus lovingly taught them the way of the kingdom by healing them. As the day faded, Jesus used the physical needs of the people to emphasize spiritual lessons as he performed a miracle of providing an abundance of food for all the people from one kid's lunch.

Of course the primary lesson is that Jesus is the Bread of Life, and we should feed on him by seeking to know and appropriate his marvelous salvation in our life. (see John 6). Yet there's something else Jesus was trying to show his disciples. When his disciples presented the crisis need for food he said, "You give them something to eat" (Matt. 14:16 ESV)!

Why did he say that? To tease them? Of course not! He knew they didn't have food for all those people. He was speaking spiritually while they were thinking physically. He was saying, *You need to start being like me and instructing in the way of life! You give them some spiritual nourishment through all the teaching you've heard and know! It's time to start continuing my ministry.* And he says that to all of us. All of his disciples and especially men need to hear, "You give them something to eat"!

I am in no way calling men to rise up against leadership or the established rule God has instituted for his church. He has placed leadership in the church to which we need to submit and give honor. But, man, you have the privilege and opportunity to get there, no matter who you are or where you come from. Pursue leadership in the church with a passion, whether you're educated, uneducated, blue-collar or white, wealthy or barely able to make ends meet. That's your call, and you should acquire the traits, character, and knowledge of a leader. It's not going to happen overnight; it will take years, but your church should encourage you to get going! If it doesn't, find one that does.

Finally, while we give instruction to our families and in the church, we should also be giving it to the world. The world needs to know the ways of God and the way of Christ, whether it wants to follow or not. It's not our job to enforce it. We are called to be a witness, a light in the darkness, to fearlessly give out the truth and the gospel when we're able, regardless of the outcome.

It's not always easy, as you know. The world is increasingly hostile toward us telling it anything. We can hardly declare something to be right or wrong in today's society without an uproar, being ostracized, losing our jobs, or worse. But guess what? As men, we still need to speak up. Declare what's right and true! We need to go against the flow and open our mouths when God calls us to. We're going to need what's coming next to do that!

A.R.I.S.E.

S—STRENGTH

*Being a Christian isn't for sissies, It takes a real man to live
for God—a lot more man than to live for the devil.
If you wanna live right these days you gotta be tough.*

Johnny Cash

*Masculinity is not something given to you, something you're born
with, but something you gain. And you gain it
by winning small battles with honor.*

Norman Mailer

CHAPTER 8

WON'T BACK DOWN

A spectacular natural phenomenon is the now-endangered Coho and Chinook salmon of northwestern America. After birth and staying for one to two years in the freshwater streambeds of Idaho, they make their way toward the coast and out to the ocean. Miraculously they are able to adapt to saltwater, where they live for four to five years, gaining mass and strength. Then suddenly an internal instinct, a sort of homing device attributed to a magnetic field, calls them to migrate back to their place of birth in the fall to reproduce. So, migrating with millions of other salmon, they begin their journey back upstream and inland eight hundred or so miles to spawn in the streambeds of their birth. It's during these salmon runs that they hurl themselves up rushing waterfalls, up steep rapids, over rocks, and hopefully past hungry bears as well as man-made dams with amazing strength for the sake of bringing forth new life. Many don't make it, and those that do die after spawning. It's an incredible display of strength and resolve.

Once you have committed to being a spiritual leader in the home, the church, and the world, you have begun your journey upstream to promote life! You are now swimming against the natural flow of the world. You are fighting the forces of darkness and the devil, who influences the ways of society and fallen man. Now more than ever, as you seek to take a stand and speak up for righteousness and truth, you will experience the spiritual foes of evil coming against you. But take courage, for as Jesus has promised, "I have overcome the world" (John 16:33, NLT). In Christ we are "more than conquerors" (Rom. 8:37, ESV) because "greater is He who is in you than he who is in the world" (1 John 4:4, NASB).

We need only to engage and stay on that journey upstream. Before long we will see the good effects come about in our sphere of influence. This requires strength and fortitude, which brings us to the S in ARISE: Show *strength* and courage in the walk of faith and truth.

God is looking for strong men. Upstreamers!

Be strong in the Lord and in the strength of His might. (Eph. 6:10, NASB)

Act like men, be strong. (1 Cor. 16:13, NASB)

Men are needed to show strength by standing up
to the darkness as the rooster crows to ward off any
predators, such as snakes and hawks, to protect their roosts.
We have to be strong to face adversity and bear assaults
as the apostle Paul did—and as Jesus did—to continue
advancing the kingdom of God and his truth against the
flow of the evil in this world. Additionally, strength is
needed to not retaliate in any way to abuses or contempt
toward us, but respond in a kind and loving manner and
turn the cheek. Paul wrote, "Take your share of suffering
as a good soldier of Jesus Christ" (2 Tim. 2:3, NLV).

Actually, a good way to develop that strength is by
instructing our families in the way of the Lord. As we are
diligent to teach and run our homes in a God-honoring
way, we will face conflict and challenges, from the two-
year-old's temper tantrums to the slammed doors of those
blessed middle-schoolers, to the outright rebellion of
teenagers escaping out bedroom windows after curfew.
This is a training ground to learn how to be strong
and uphold a righteous standard in a controlled, loving
manner. It's an environment where your faith is tested,
and you learn to trust God that blessing will come later as
you stand against sin, even though at the present it seems
as though all hell is breaking loose!

Don't despise your parenting/leadership role when
it gets tough and you get fed up because you can't even
watch the game! Hang in there. It makes you strong as a
spiritual leader and brings blessing to your children.

★★★

We men are typically drawn to appreciate great feats of strength. It's just the way we are, whether it's winning in athletics, becoming a business icon and building an empire, or as an artist avoiding the pressure of commercialism and risking to create something new, which ends up being a huge success. We love it. The movie *13 Hours: The Secret Soldiers of Benghazi* (which contains some graphic violence), wonderfully displays the great courage those men took in risking their lives and careers to do what was right, to save those at an American diplomatic compound, which was an amazing feat!

If there's one area in which we men like to show we're better than women it's in physical strength. If you're old enough or if you've come across him on YouTube, you'll remember the outrageous comedy of the now-deceased comic and actor Andy Kaufman. One of his claims to fame was being the "Inter-Gender Wrestling Champion of the World." He went around to nightclubs to wrestle, saying he could beat any woman any time and eventually ended up doing so on national television. It was so politically incorrect, shameful, and ugly. Some say the whole thing was staged, but either way it was hilarious, and emphasized the truth that we guys like it to be known we're stronger than the gals.

Men have an average of 72.6 pounds of muscle compared to women, who have 46.2 pounds. Men have 40 percent more muscle mass in the upper body, and 33 percent more in the lower body. Average height for men is five feet, ten inches, compared to women, who average five feet, four inches according to Livestrong.com.

These differences suggest something, as the physical realm often mirrors the spiritual. Men are reminded by their physique, deep voices, and natural boldness that they are to be strong in *spirit* as well. They should be powerful in conviction, resolve, confidence, self-possession, and heart. These God-given qualities and traits are good, as they help us lead in the way of faith and truth.

Be aware, however, the world wants us to feel ashamed of our strength. The world and our society imply now that it's improper to display the natural male characteristics of strength, and we need to suppress them. Men are made out to be arrogant and disruptive if they are bold or strong in self-possession and conviction. The acceptable form of manhood now is the feminized man. You'll notice the new Hollywood male is often portrayed on screen as scared and incapable which is quite a departure from John Wayne! Desirable men are those who don't make trouble and are soft and unassuming. This push for the "new male" is the way feminist agendas can continue to be promoted.

Yet men's strength is the reason for a lot of what's good in the world. We shouldn't be ashamed or afraid of it. As author John Eldredge says, "Many of us are unnerved by our own masculinity, afraid that if you let it show you'll do something bad!" That's what we've been taught and have learned from the media.

Strength is a good thing as long as we're seeking to live for God. He wants us to use it for him and the advancement of his purposes. Be strong, be bold, and don't be ashamed of it.

Some of us have seen our fathers abuse their strength on us or on others we love, and we swore we would never do that to anyone else. And so we run from exhibiting any kind of strength. But it's just like anything else. The abuse of credit cards leading to monstrous debt doesn't make credit cards bad; they can be extremely helpful for traveling and keeping track of expenses. Sleeping around with various partners can wreak havoc in people's lives with kids born out of wedlock, disease and broken families—but that doesn't make sex bad! It's the abuse of sex and immorality that causes disaster. It's the same with strength. If you've condemned the use of strength because you have seen it misused and cause harm, don't dismiss it as something never to display. Instead, redeem it and seek to use it for good purposes. Use it for God.

When Joshua was about to lead the children of Israel into the promised land, what did God say to him? "Be strong and of good courage"! (Josh. 1:6, 9, NKJV).

The historical event recorded in the Bible of the nation of Israel entering the promised land and conquering its territory, is a wonderful depiction of how to live out the new life in Christ and obtain God's blessings. It represents the advancing of the kingdom of God by overcoming evil and establishing a witness of God in our world.

We have to be "strong and courageous" and fight for it, just like the children of Israel, because the enemies of darkness don't want this to happen. They don't want to lose any territory or lose their dominant influence on people and in the world. They want to keep us, and the kingdom of light out from gaining any ground and drive us back into the wilderness wasteland.

God needs us to be strong. And we can; it's in us or rather *he's* in us:, "I can do all things through Christ which strengthens me"(Phil 4:13, NKJV) Our Joshua, Jesus, will lead us through to victory if we act strong and are willing to engage in the battle against this dark evil and not back down.

A key characteristic for living a victorious Christian life, making an impact on others, experiencing blessings, and achieving great glory for God is strength! We have to learn to be strong in our spirits with resolve, strong in faith and truth, believing in and upholding the ways of God in our own lives and in the lives of our families. Then we declare those ways to the world. Those are the types of muscles God wants us to flex and not be ashamed of.

Now let's see how to get the spiritual protein to build those muscles.

Like the rock that was smitten, we too need to be broken,
before the rivers of blessing can flow out through us to others.
The opposition of men and their false accusations
serve to keep us broken before God.

Zac Poonen

In my deepest wound I saw your glory, and it dazzled me.

Augustine of Hippo

I like criticism. It makes you strong.

LeBron James

CHAPTER 9

BUILDING SPIRITUAL MUSCLE

Steroids are synonymous with everything that's bad in sports. Who can forget the letdown of Mark McGwire or Alex Rodriguez, record-setting home-run hitters, when busted for using performance-enhancing drugs?! Or of Lance Armstrong being stripped of all his Tour de France titles after having being caught doping? Unfortunately there's a lot of it still going on due to the advances in how to hide it with sophisticated methods, such as injecting with a tattoo needle, which the body can adjust to and regulate more easily.

But of course the question that automatically comes to mind is, why would someone want to achieve success knowing he cheated, even if he didn't get caught? It's a fake victory!

Careful now—don't get too self-righteous. If you think about it, don't we all do the same with our lives? We tend to become strong, confident, and self-assured, gaining validation from others through false methods—do we not? Whether it's success in our careers, higher education, financial status, big house in the nice part of town, looks, a pretty wife, family heritage, people's approval, self-righteousness, religiousness, or lots of followers on Twitter: They're all fake sources of strength. They're spiritual steroids! They're not the real strength God is looking for in his men. We're feeling strong and confident for all the wrong reasons.

Yet we all go for those things naturally, and the Lord has to go to work breaking us to expose the "doping" we do so we can develop true strength. True strength in the spiritual realm has much more power than the man-made, synthesized stuff.

God's gym is the way of brokenness. If you work out or can remember from health class in school, for muscles to grow, they must first be broken down. That's why you lift weights. In breaking down the muscle tissue it then heals and grows back stronger. The same principle applies to spiritual muscle. The goal of spiritual leaders is to move in the strength of relying on God and believing in the high position we have in Christ, not in how successful we are in our earthly pursuits.

So he breaks us. Sickness, financial ruin, loss of job, broken dreams, family fallouts—whatever it is, God uses them to tear down the old ways of strength, self-assurance, and self-confidence, so the real power can come out—him!

H. A. Ironside, former pastor of Moody Church in Chicago, proclaimed, "God is looking for broken men who have judged themselves in the light of the cross of Christ. When He wants anything done, He takes up men who have come to the end of themselves, whose confidence is not in themselves, but in God."

Author and preacher Vance Havner also described it quite visually: "God uses broken things. It takes broken soil to produce a crop, broken clouds to give rain, broken grain to give bread, broken bread to give strength. It is the broken alabaster box that gives forth perfume. It is Peter, weeping bitterly, who returns to greater power than ever."

Having a willingness to be broken is based on the foundational principle of the Christian faith—carrying our cross! "Then Jesus told his disciples, 'If any of you wants to be my follower, you must give up your own way, take up your cross, and follow me. If you try to hang on to your life, you will lose it. But if you give up your life for my sake, you will save it" (Matt. 16:24–25, NLT). A good popular definition of carrying our cross is, a commitment to God to the point of giving up our hopes and dreams, our possessions, our rights, even our very life if need be, to follow him and his plan for us.

As God's man, we need to lead the way and set this example. We can't become an authentic spiritual leader without it. We have to be resolute and strong in picking up our cross, like Jesus, who gave up everything when he carried his. He gave up his right to be recognized and honored as God, as well as acting out in his infinite power anytime he wanted to, and a whole lot more! Let us as his followers also be willing to give up our treasured things we hold on to that make us feel valued and significant.

By carrying our cross God does his marvelous work to rid us of our self-life, and for Christ's life to grow and flow out of us. Watchman Nee declared in *Release of the Spirit*: "It is vital that we be broken by the Lord; his life is imprisoned in us. The motive behind all of God's orderings is to destroy our outward man. Once this occurs, the Spirit can come forth."

Of course we go kicking and screaming! It feels like we're dying because self-denial goes against everything we naturally love. But trust God; he's taking you somewhere amazing to be a powerful spiritual leader, with his life flowing through you. And as with Job, the patriarch who watched his life crumble before his eyes (see Job 42:12), God will restore us with much more after he strips away what we've been holding on to instead of him.

A. W. Tozer in his timeless classic *Pursuit of God* affirms, "Insist that the work (of the cross) be done. The cross is rough, and it is deadly, but it is effective. It does not leave its victim hanging there forever. There comes a moment when its work is finished and the suffering victim dies. After that is resurrection glory and power, and the pain is forgotten, for the joy of the veil is taken away and we have entered in actual spiritual experience, (to) the presence of the living God."

The second reason for the need to carry our cross and the willingness to be broken is that it teaches us how the kingdom advances. Jesus, who inaugurated and brought in the kingdom of God, did so by his death, and he left us with a principle.

In speaking the truth to influence others to live in a way that honors God and follow Christ, there will often be a dying of self-need, a moment of risking and experiencing rejection or condemnation, whether it be a screaming teenager for grounding her, a co-worker's scorn for not leaving work early with them since the boss isn't there, or simply ridicule for telling someone about the way of salvation.

This "dying" is how the power of God and his Spirit is released from us, having a powerful effect on others, just as Jesus' death did and still does. "When I am lifted up from the earth (on the cross), will draw all people to myself (John 12:32, AMP).

In our natural world, dying is weakness. It's the ultimate loss. But in the spiritual realm "soul-death" that comes from being a witness of the truth against the darkness results in divine strength, resurrection power, and the Spirit of God flowing out of us! We need to become convinced of this, as it is imperative for the kingdom of God to advance. It is why the apostle Paul said, "When I am weak, then I am strong" (2 Cor. 12:10, ESV) and encouraged us to be "always carrying about in the body the death of Jesus that the life of Jesus also may be manifested in our bodies" (2 Cor. 4:10, ESV).

When we are humble and courageously carry our cross, allowing the breaking and dying of ourselves—whether on a large or small scale—the Spirit of God and his power begins to flow out of us! God is coming out, drawing others to himself and bringing blessing. This is true strength and how the kingdom of God spreads.

If you remember the end of *Indiana Jones and the Last Crusade,* Indiana had to reach the fountain of life and bring back water to save his father, who had been shot. But the entryway was guarded by a mechanism so that all who tried to enter lost their heads! So as Indy advanced he used a clue given to him by his father: "Only the penitent man shall pass." The mechanism was tripped when Indy approached and he was about to encounter the same fate as those who tried before, but at the last second he dropped to the floor, displaying humility and penitence. He survived the test and eventually made it to where the fountain of life was to give to his father.

It is only when we are humbled and brought low, not depending on our own strength, that we are brought close to God and used by him with power to bless others. Of Jesus Hebrews 12:2 (NLT) says, "Because of the joy awaiting him, he endured the cross, disregarding its shame." Often when I'm encountering a cross moment I start to complain in my heart to God. *Why, Lord?!* But he's doing something good, which will ultimately bring blessing to us, and others. Trust him and be strong in enduring it. Disregard the shame, knowing there is good coming from it.

You can see a great example of this kind of spiritual breaking that results in blessing with David, just before he finally was anointed king. In the second half of the book of 1 Samuel you find him hiding out on the outskirts of the land of Israel and in the land of the Philistines, running from King Saul. While dwelling in Ziglag, a town in Philistine territory, he and his men arrived home from a journey to find their city burned with fire and all their wives and kids taken by the Amalekites, another pagan enemy.

The men were overcome with grief and sorrow, wept loudly, and wanted to kill David, their leader, for allowing this to happen—a serious cross moment for him! But the scripture says, "David strengthened himself in the LORD" (1 Sam. 30:6, NASB). This enabled him to regroup and track down the Amalekites, make a surprise raid, and wipe them out with a great slaughter. And he recovered all the families that were taken. Additionally he acquired a great abundance of goods and booty from the raid, some of which he offered to the elders of Judah back in Israel, so they would receive him and he could begin his reign as king there. God had a plan to promote his kingdom, and it took David going through a difficult time of weakness to make it happen.

God powerfully does his work in and around us when we carry our cross. Some of us have grown weary of dying to self, and have slid the cross off our shoulders onto the ground. If we only knew the blessings we were missing out on! Let's have the courage to pick it up again and see the marvelous things God will do in our life.

★★★

How do you think David "strengthened himself in the LORD" in the midst of these dire circumstances? He hoped in God. He believed and trusted in his mercy. He reminded himself that God loved him and was still in control. He probably felt guilty for living in the Philistine territory and pretending he was loyal to their king, but he relied on the forgiveness, goodness, grace, and favor of God.

This is a great example showing us how to get strength to carry our cross. We must always believe who we are in Christ now: We are one with him, seated with him at the right hand of God (See Eph. 2:6). We are in the same cherished position that the Son has before the Father, favored and loved, doted on the way parents do with their only child (See Eph. 1:6). And in Christ we have overcome, and will overcome everything evil that happens to us.

That's how our true inner strength is developed and why the apostle Paul said, "I can do all things through [Christ] who strengthens me" (Phil. 4:19, ESV). Next time you feel inadequate, insignificant, weak, condemned, or fearful, renewing your mind to the realities in Christ and believing them will strengthen you.

Finally, here are a few other sources of spiritual proteins: Of course reading the Word of God to become aware of our blessings in Christ, as just mentioned, makes us strong. 1 John 2:14 (ESV) states: "I have written to you young men because you are strong, and the Word of God abides in you, and you have overcome the evil one."

Retreating to a private place for prayer also strengthens us, as it did Jesus in the garden before he went to the cross (Luke 22:43). The result of prayer is to remind us who God is, and who we are before him amidst life's circumstances—that he loves us and is in control.

And believe it or not, partaking of the Lord's Supper where we remember the Lord for what he did for us also has a strengthening effect. As we feed on the love of

Christ coming from heaven (bread), and his death for us (wine), it reminds us symbolically that we have died and are now alive in Christ. By feeding on those truths and worshipping him we get strong! Martyn Lloyd-Jones says, "The Lord's Supper strengthens us, giving us vigor and life, and we take of Him."

Fellowship with other believers strengthens us and especially fellowship with other men who are also on the road pursuing spiritual leadership. There are times when you'll feel like all the world is against you, even your family. That's why God gave us the church, to give us the love and fellowship we need to continue on. It's much harder to go it alone. Don't forsake the church and find other men who are going through these same experiences to strengthen and encourage each other.

Carrying our cross and believing who we are in Christ are the spiritual proteins needed to ARISE and display real strength. A regular dose of these will result in becoming an influential spiritual leader.

You cannot possess your promised land without a battle.

Sunday Adelaja

The road to the promised land runs past Sinai. The moral law may exist to be transcended: but there is no transcending it for those who have not first admitted its claims up on them, and then tried with all their strength to meet that claim, and fairly and squarely faced the fact of their failure.

C.S. Lewis

The kingdom of heaven suffers violent assault, and violent men seize it by force [as a precious prize].

Jesus Christ

CHAPTER 10

THE RIGHT FIGHT

Paradise. That's what you call it when you see construction start on a new house on a vacant lot across the street from where you live and you're six years old. Big mounds of dirt, deep holes, cut-down trees, wooden planks like drawbridges over trenches up to cinderblock foundations: sublime! It's as if God saw you were bored and dropped a perfect playground for boys from heaven right in your front yard.

My cousin and I were having the time of our lives jumping off the mountains of dirt one spring afternoon when we heard young voices emerging from the woods behind us. Billy, the annoying kid from down the street, and his brother also were exploring with excitement their newfound utopia. Well, true to the nature of young boys and in classic *Lord of the Flies* form, within minutes we were telling each other to go home as this was our turf and ours alone.

As I took a stand atop our mound proclaiming territorial rights, the first rock whizzed past my head. The battle was on! My cousin and I crouched below our mound of dirt and hurled rocks over their mound, shielding ourselves with one of those plastic toboggans left over from the winter that I grabbed from my front yard.

I still can remember the thrill of doing what every boy is told not to do by his mother: throwing rocks at kids and fighting against these invaders with my cousin. Then I pulled up from behind our shield with rocks in each hand ready to unload and BAM! It hit me! Incoming artillery found my right eye, knocking me backward, sending me running for my front door crying out for Momma as the blood trickled down my face. It left me with a nice shiner for my kindergarten class picture that year.

Perhaps the scolding for throwing rocks hurt just as much as the rock, or maybe it was the fact that I grew up during the Vietnam War and always heard about the killings and other bad things about that war. Or perhaps it was just the fact that I grew up in a family of six with a strict father where no fighting was tolerated. Whatever the cause, I came to believe conflict was bad. I should avoid it at all costs. And if it happened it was because I was doing something wrong.

On top of that, due to the legalistic leanings of my childhood church, I had adopted an erroneous worldview that said if I tried hard to live perfectly righteous, God would not allow much conflict in my life. He would make it mostly smooth sailing. Boy, did I come crashing down from that worldview in my first pastorate! I quickly learned that when you promote the kingdom of God, the forces of darkness rear their ugly heads, no matter how perfectly you try to live. And ironically I found out that if you're doing things right and living according to the will of God, it's inevitable that you will face opposition and struggle at times.

Conflict. It's here—the battle between good and evil, truth and lies, hope and despair, rage against the hearts and souls of mankind. It's not just something in the movies. If you choose to ignore it and just get on with your life of merely making money, achieving success, and looking for the next good time, you are losing the battle. If you engage in advancing truth, goodness, light, and hope for yourself and others around you, you will experience the fight.

For years I did not want to be in the fight. I just wanted to have a good time and be friends with everybody! Being in the music business I developed an *everybody has to like me* mindset, so I went AWOL as a Christian soldier for a while. But if you want to be a true man of God—if you're going to ARISE and be an impacting spiritual leader, you can't make being popular and adored your goal. Life will involve conflict and the Lord wants us to be sober-minded about it (1 Thess. 5:8).

We must realize we're at spiritual war! Don't numb yourself to it—that's the devil's tactic to make you dismiss the reality of the battle. If all is peaceful in your life all the time, you're actually getting bombed heavily. You've been ambushed and taken out! John Eldredge is quoted as saying "Until you understand that you were born into a world at war, you'll believe some pretty awful things about God."

God fights against the darkness, and he wants us as men to join him. "The LORD is a man of war; the LORD is his name" (Exod. 15:3, ESV).

Of course we're talking spiritually here, not physically. Paul wrote to the church at Corinth in Greece about 57AD: "We use God's mighty weapons, not worldly weapons, to knock down the strongholds of human reasoning and to destroy false arguments. We destroy every proud obstacle that keeps people from knowing God. We capture their rebellious thoughts and teach them to obey Christ." (2 Cor. 10:4–5, NTL).

★★★

The fight is against sin that the devil and the powers of darkness want to enslave us in and blind us from understanding the truth of the knowledge of God. They don't want us to experience the new reality found in Jesus and obtain its blessings, so they come against us in many ways.

As I mentioned previously, the historical event that occurred when the nation of Israel came out of slavery in Egypt and into the promised land is really a lesson for us in our Christian journey. After crossing the Red Sea and traveling through the wilderness, the Israelites came to the edge of that land and found there were many enemy nations occupying it. For the Israelites to take it, they would have to go in and fight.

The first time they came to the border, they sent twelve spies to survey the land (see Num. 13–14). Only two of the spies, Joshua and Caleb, said, "Let's do it! We've got this with the help of the Lord." But the other ten spies said, "We will perish if we go fight them. They have fortified cities with giants!" They did not want to fight, and their voices prevailed among the people, so Israel turned around and wandered in the wilderness for forty years. After that disbelieving generation died off, the new generation came along, and they entered the land. They fought, kicked out the pagan nations, and occupied it.

What God has offered us through Christ will involve conflict and a fight, requiring *strength,* faith, and courage, just like it did for the children of Israel, but it brings great reward and blessing. Jesus has promised us the victory. "Thanks be to God who gives us the victory through Jesus Christ our Lord," (1 Cor. 15:57, NASB).

As spiritual leaders we must fight to realize that victory, and claim the territory of more blessings. "God invites us to enter the promised land" writes Max Lucado in his *Glory Days,* "but to do that, we must turn our backs on the wilderness. "Wilderness mentality says I'm weak, [promised land takers] say I was weak, but I'm getting stronger."

Paul wrote to Timothy, who appears to have been backing off from the supernatural struggle, "Fight the good fight of the faith [in the conflict with evil]; take hold of the eternal life to which you were called" (1 Tim 6:12, AMP). God has qualified us to be in the battle on the side of light and truth the day we received Christ. We're in his army, "Onward, Christian soldier, marching as to war," as the classic hymn goes.

This battle is mainly fought on two fronts. The first is pretty apparent, which is fighting against sin and evil in our own life, and in the lives of those under our care and sphere of influence. Things like immorality, lying, cheating, drunkenness, coveting, slander, pride, hypocrisy, selfishness, and so on. We fight to push out those enemies from taking up residence in our life, and in others.

The second area is with the heart and mind. It's fought against the lies and blindness the powers of darkness want to keep us in so that we won't come into light of truth and the gospel, or more truth about Jesus and increased blessing. As Martyn Lloyd-Jones says in his exposition on Ephesians, "This is a battle that has to be in a spiritual manner and with spiritual understanding. The battle rages to keep you and me in darkness as slaves that we might not apprehend the saving power of the gospel."

I wrote a song a while back called "The Right Fight." The chorus goes like this: "There's a battle raging that takes all my might, and the way to fight the battle is faith in the truth of all I have in you Lord . . . this is the Right Fight."

Now sins strengthen belief in the lies and darken our understanding; they cause blindness in us, (see Eph. 4:18–19). And the more blindness and lies believed, the more we sin. It's a nasty cycle that only God's light of revelation can break.

"For God who said let light shine out of darkness has shone in our hearts to give the light of the knowledge of the glory of God in the face of Jesus" (2 Cor. 4:6, ESV).

As Christians we have light and are not in darkness like unbelievers. And although the light can never go out, it can get dim from the heavy cloud of sin in our life. And so we fight this battle, first in our own life and then in the lives of others.

Jesus said, "You are light of the world" (Matt. 5:14, ESV). And with that light, as God's representatives and a good rooster, we help open the eyes of people to the salvation of Jesus, warning them of the harm of sin that keeps them in darkness and brings destruction. We shine the light and fight against the lies that people believe in.

At times when we're faithfully advancing the kingdom of light in our family or out in the world, the devil will do all he can to make us stop—from broken down cars, to lost business deals, sickness, crashing computers, and the like. He'll also bombard us with a host of doubting thoughts to make us fearful and cripple us so we don't keep going. Hang on and press through! There's blessing waiting! You will overcome if you resist, stay strong, and not turn back. That's why we have that great metaphor of putting on the armor of God in Ephesians 6:10–11 (ESV): "Finally, be strong in the Lord and in the strength of his might. Put on the whole armor of God, that you may be able to stand against the schemes of the devil."

Through renewing our minds with the truth of Jesus from scripture, we come to believe we're good, a part of Christ, loved, and totally forgiven. We trust that God's good, and he's got a plan, and by pressing on will overcome and receive blessing. The armor allows us to take the hit of circumstances and bad treatment by people, and keep going. This is what Jesus did—Jesus, who was exalted with great glory and brought us immense blessing—the ultimate spiritual leader! That's why we're to keep our eyes on Christ, understand how he did it, and follow.

> "[Look] to Jesus, the founder and perfecter of our faith, who for the joy that was set before him endured the cross, despising the shame, and is seated at the right hand of the throne of God" (Heb. 12:2, ESV).

The battle is waiting for you to engage, to ARISE, with all resources of strength necessary so you don't get knocked out, give up, and retreat from the conflict, (and go running to your mother!) The question is, will you engage?

God is better served in resisting temptation to evil,
than in many formal prayers.

William Penn

We gain the strength of the temptation we resist.

Ralph Waldo Emerson

God clearly showed me that I needed to be a submissive wife if I
wanted to be effective in ministry. The truth is, if we don't learn
to submit to authority, we won't ever learn to submit to God.

Joyce Meyer

CHAPTER 11

CAR ACCIDENTS IN YOUR DRIVEWAY

On D-Day when the Allied troops were deployed to capture the beaches of Normandy, many soldiers didn't even get to fire a shot. The boats coming off the ships with solders were bombarded by enemy fire from the high cliffs while approaching the shoreline. If you've ever seen the movie *Saving Private Ryan,* you know it was a pretty graphic scene on Omaha Beach. After much training, paratroopers seeking to drop in behind enemy lines were picked off by antiaircraft and artillery fire before they even landed. Fortunately, despite heavy losses and casualties, Normandy was captured, giving a foothold to liberate France and eventually bring down the German regime overtaking Europe.

Too many guys have the intent and passion to make changes in their lives so they can make a difference in this world by guiding others in the way of life and blessing, but as on D-day they hardly begin before being taken out by the enemy. It's like pulling out of your driveway and having a car accident! They're losing the fight in their own lives and in their own backyard, disqualifying them from having greater areas of influence and more blessing. Remember what Jesus said: "He who is faithful in a very little thing is faithful also in much" (Luke 16:10, NASB).

And I think you know what's tripping up a lot of guys: wocka-wocka, gland-to-gland combat, jumpin' bones, whatever you want to call it: out-of-bounds sex! Strong men of God who do great things for him have this under control and are not in bondage to desires or lusts. It's what a true man is, and the key to success. And God will test you on it, more than once, before making you a prominent spiritual leader. How many men have fallen and ruined their lives and careers as well as caused great hurt and harm to others because of untamed lusts.

The whole golf industry took a hit because of Tiger Woods's improprieties. Many congregations have suffered greatly because of fallen pastors. America groaned with shame with the whole Bill Clinton scandal. And down through history kingdoms and civilizations have fallen because of uncontrolled libidos.

Lust begins to be a problem when men are young. We have to teach our young men to develop strength in this so they take it through their whole lives. It starts with guarding them against the barrage of sexually explicit programs that kids are often exposed to and teaching them to turn from these as well. Their early exposure stirs up interest way before they're even close to being adults and often ends in perversion. Fight to keep your kids from watching garbage as long as possible.

Some PG-13 movies push the boundaries too far and should be R-rated. I would always keep it PG unless you know for certain there's no suggestive material in a PG-13. There are good Christian websites that can do prescreening for you (such as crosswalk.com and pluggedin.com). My mother and father always monitored what I was taking in well into my late teens (my mom would throw out the suggestive magazines that came in the mail!), which helped me not to succumb to the temptation of premarital sex.

Young men develop leadership and strength before they're married by learning to be strong against sexual temptation. It's easier to establish yourself as a credible spiritual leader with authority in the home if you have not succumbed to the pressures of premarital sex. Your wife will respect you for it right out of the gate. If you have sex outside of marriage before you're married, a wife may secretly wonder if you'll also have sex outside of marriage after you're married.

In our guidance with our children and especially boys, we must not make them feel ashamed for their God-given sex drive. Always remind them it's a good thing, but the way we act on it is what is right or wrong.

But how can we influence our boys in the way of purity if we aren't seeking it ourselves? If we're to redeem manhood and make it something desirable again, this is foundational. It's why we have so many spiritually weak men in our country. We've dropped our guard with the sexual thoughts and images we expose ourselves to and have made a mess of things, we must get strong again in fighting against its hold in our lives. When you succumb to sexual temptation, you give your strength away. You lose the ability to ARISE and be a warrior who fights and overcomes the darkness.

Proverbs 5:7–9 (NLV) states plainly: "Now then, my sons, listen to me. Do not turn away from the words of my mouth. Keep far away from [the wayward woman]. Do not go near the door of her house. If you do, you would give your strength to others, and your years to those without loving-kindness."

Also to experience more of the presence with God and get close with him, we need a clear conscience. When you're sinning, the Lord is still with you, but your conscience is guilty and your natural response is to hide from God, the way Adam and Eve did after they sinned. You lose your boldness to draw near to him. Don't miss out on cultivating a powerful presence of God in your life thinking about or toying with illicit sex.

If you're not satisfied sexually in your marriage, it's time to work on that relationship to make it good again. Get some help. The physical is representative of the relational. Don't ignore the problem and look elsewhere, especially not at porn. Dr. Archibald Hart rightfully declares, "There's no greater threat to a healthy or sanctified male sexuality than pornography." A study conducted by the Barna Group reports that 68 percent of Christian men view porn, which is the same rate as for secular men. Google Research reports that porn sites receive more traffic than Netflix, Amazon, and Twitter combined! And according to Webroot, marriage infidelity has increased 300 percent because of it.

This is serious warfare that we can't ignore! In God's eyes, viewing porn leading to sexual fantasies is like committing those acts. When you look on a woman with lust in your mind, you've committed the act in your heart (Matt. 5:28). Boom! What you see and think about is what you're driven to do. And what's coming down the pike with virtual sex will make it even worse. In order to be an effective spiritual leader, you have to forsake it and break free of this once and for all—and we can. We can get the victory if we want it through Jesus. Many men have.

Look what Job said. Job was the man of God who lived thousands of years ago whom God thought a lot of and revealed himself to intimately. He was a man whose life continues to have great spiritual influence on people to this day! Job said,

"I made a covenant with my eyes not to look with lust at a young woman" (Job 31:1, ESV). I like Steve Arterburn's approach as mentioned in his book *Every Man's Battle: Winning the War on Sexual Temptation*: "Let all sexual appetites and desires be fulfilled by your wife and your wife only."

For some this will feel like a great loss: *What do I live for now if I take that away?* Sexual immorality and porn addition are heart issues. There's an ache, a void, an emptiness that needs to be satisfied and filled, and either what Jesus offers is far better, or it's not! Someone once said we won't leave our idols till we find something better. There is something much better. However, we don't get to enjoy the spiritual blessings of the kingdom, which we're a part of now, when we're indulging in our lusts (Ephesians 5:5).

In those painful moments of desire when you want to indulge in something on a website or be extra friendly with that attractive secretary, deny it, turn to the Lord in your heart, and pray. Ask him to reveal more of what he has given you in salvation and to be full with the Holy Spirit who gives joy, life, power, and peace. If you're serious he will answer that prayer! As Christian counselor Dr. Chuck Lynch says, "Don't seek to change your mood by indulging in porn or other temptations and fantasies, but ask the Spirit to change how you feel."

In your downtime or while driving, let your mind be taken up with pursuing the truth in Jesus and understanding it better rather than wander-lusting about some scantily clad woman. Listen to good Christian music to get you thinking about higher things.

You'll find experiencing what Jesus offers in salvation is far superior. But we won't come into it flirting with immorality. What we sacrifice by being in bondage to these lusts is a great loss, and they never bring true satisfaction anyway. You are always left needing more.

Having Jesus' presence, the fullness of the Holy Spirit in you, and being his leader for others offers something so much better. You will begin to taste eternal life, which genuinely satisfies. As Paul wrote to his young protégé Timothy, "Fight the good fight of the faith. Take hold of the eternal life to which you were called" (1 Tim. 6:12 ESV).

Take the first step of faith and decide to put away sexual addictions now. In doing so, the presence of Jesus will become real and powerful in you, and the Lord will put you on the front lines to fight against evil. Knowing you have the strength to win the battles, and help save others, bringing blessing to all. Here is a few resources to get you started:

www.covenanteyes.com—Software accountability for computer and phone

Every Man's battle: Winning the War on Sexual Temptation One Victory at a Time by Stephen Aterburn

Conquerseries.com : Battle Plan for purity Action-packed DVD teaching

★★★

The other area where we need to show strength in before having a greater influence and more territory in the kingdom of God as a spiritual leader is establishing loving rule in our families. As mentioned in chapter 2, God has placed the man at the head of the home, and we must start showing leadership there. Let's take a look at how.

Something happened back in the seventies, when being a cool dad was all that mattered. If you were a mother or father who taught respect and honor for parents, you were a drag! If a dad sought to maintain order over his home by setting boundaries and establishing rules, he was out of it and old-fashioned. A cool dad let kids do whatever they want. And I believe that was the start of the dismantling of the home in the modern age.

I can remember hearing stories (the seventies were a little before my time) about high school kids back then addressing their parents and other parents by their first names and hanging out with them as their buddies. Of course TV programmers picked up on this and ran with it, and they're still doing so to this day.

If Hollywood is not making fathers look like dorks and fools, then it's making them easygoing, supercool, and irrelevant, careful to not act with any kind of authority. And after years of this constant reprogramming of how a "good" dad should be, men have bought into it and ceased trying to establish any kind of authority in the home. It's just another attack on the leadership of man and against God and his design that glorifies him.

Dr. Ken Leaman writes in *How to have a new kid by Friday*, It all comes down to who really is in charge of your family. Is it you or your child? Today's parents often don't act like parents, they are so concerned about being their child's friend and making sure their child is happy and successful that they fail in their most important role: to be a parent. Mom and Dad have become mere servants rather than parents who have the child's long-term best interest in mind. As a result kids are growing more and more powerful. They are all about "me-me-me" and "gimme" and rarely considering others before themselves because they've never been taught to think that way. They are held accountable less and have fewer responsibilities in the home.

★★★

It's a man's job to bring the kids up right. While it's mom's job too, and she may be more involved day to day, he's behind it all. As I mentioned earlier in chapter 6, men are to lead in instructing their children, yet what I'm referring to here is letting kids know you are in charge, that they're ultimately accountable to you. And so it's your job to enforce the boundaries of what is acceptable and unacceptable behavior. It's not all left to mom! Because again, you're the one to give an answer to the Lord for your family. So lead lovingly, but be firm about it.

We're not doing anybody any good by just being cool. We do great harm to our kids and ourselves when we don't fulfill our role as spiritual leaders and head over our families. We can certainly be our children's friend, and we must play and have fun with them—until there's a breach of authority. You ask them to do something and they don't, or they break a rule—then you have to step up the leadership and enforce the boundaries, gently but firmly, in a controlled manner. You have God's blessing behind you to do so, and you're helping your children respect and take authority from God, which will save them.

> Don't fail to correct your children; discipline won't hurt them! . . . Punishment will keep them out of hell. (Proverbs 23:13–14, TLB)

> Reproofs for discipline are the way of life. (Proverbs 6:23, NASB)

★★★

Again, you're helping your kids listen to God in life, which will save them and land them in heaven with great glory. That's worth some uncomfortable moments with them, isn't it? It takes consistent hard work. At times you look like the bad guy, but it's so worth it! Here's the irony: You're really loving them by disciplining them. Dads who don't establish leadership and authority in the home really love themselves, not their families.

Of course, as we seek to establish leadership at home with kids, we can be direct in enforcing our rules and laying down the law, so to speak: "No, you're not gonna do that here." "You're not going to use that kinda language." "You're not allowed to go on a date alone at your age."

But with our wives, as you know, it's much different. They are our counterparts, our equals in Christ. As someone has pointed out, God took Eve from the rib of Adam, not the foot or heel. This indicates that she's alongside him as his associate and confidant. But there can't be two chiefs. It would be like having two presidents for the country, or two CEOs in a corporation: It would cause chaos and confusion.

Your wife needs to support and show the children you're the leader, that you have the ultimate responsibility before God. I've seen wives challenge and tear down men's authority in front of the kids, and it's extremely destructive.

It has to be a loving and willing regard on her part for your leadership. If your wife is defiant about your establishing any authority in the home, you have to get some counseling. Meet with an elder from the church or pastor to help work it out. You never, ever, violently enforce your authority! If you have neglected your leadership for too long, and now you're trying to reestablish it, you have to patiently help your wife see that it is the structure God intends. You probably won't accomplish this overnight. It will be a process, so pray and be patient.

And don't be a jerk! Leadership is not going around acting like a dictator or tyrant in any way. Your wife is your partner and colleague. A good president listens to his advisors, and a successful CEO relies on his staff of VPs to make good choices. They are often are more knowledgeable in specifics in areas they manage. There are many times I should have listened to my wife. God speaks often through our spouses, and if you're smart, you'll listen and always regard her and her ideas. They'll save you.

Yet, there are those times when differences arise. She thinks one way, and you're convinced God's leading the other way. Unless you're desiring to do something that's clearly sinful, it's the woman who has to back down for the sake of the authority structure, even if she's convinced you're screwing things up. And men need to be strong in holding to their conviction before the Lord and implementing their decision in the family, asking for their wives' support.

But be prepared for the fallout! Your wife isn't always going to take it too kindly, again especially if you're just beginning to establish true spiritual leadership at home. There might be some colorful words coming your way, name-calling, or the silent treatment. Don't retaliate. Be kind. You must show love here. "Hon, I know how you feel. You just have to trust me on this."

Be strong but be gentle. If you feel rejected by your wife, in your heart trust God. Pray for needed *strength* and help, and he will give it. I've done it. He knows you're trying to do what's right and establish his God-ordained authority. It won't be long before you will see whether you were correct or made a mistake. But either way, believe it or not, your wife will start to appreciate, love, and honor you more for having stepped out in leadership for the good of the family and maintained your way even to the point of her dissing you momentarily. She'll come around, and actually you'll end up closer!

Once we've established spiritual leadership in our own lives and in our homes, we qualify for greater areas of influence, including church leadership, which is a great privilege with promised extra reward. But dads and husbands, as spiritual leaders our goal is different from just running a tight ship of order using fear and strict discipline. As God wants us to eventually follow him out of love, our goal is to have the family want to follow our lead because they love us, and God. That will come if we lead in love.

A.R.I.S.E.

E—EXHIBIT LOVE

Without love our life is dark, hopeless and unsatisfying.

Mother Teresa

*Love is when the other person's happiness
is more important than your own.*

H. Jackson Brown Jr.

The degree of loving is measured by the degree of giving.

Edwin Louis Cole

CHAPTER 12

FINDING THE DEEP WELL OF LOVE

It is appropriate that what the last letter of ARISE represents is at the end. For everything that we have talked about leads up to and has this goal in mind. All our previous efforts are to bring about this result. Without this next characteristic, even if you were excellent in all of the other areas, you would fail miserably as a spiritual leader. The greatest thing, and one more area we need to be strong in is the E in ARISE: *exhibit love*. Men are to be strong in being loving—sounds incredible, doesn't it? You might think it's ridiculous; real men are supposed to be tough, rational, and self-controlled in their emotions aren't they? I thought you were trying to undo the feminization of men? Well, I am, but according to God our creator, he designed men to love and to display that love, setting the example for others to follow. We have a lot of heart and shouldn't be afraid of it!

Interestingly, men are more emotional than you might think. They seem to have a more difficult time, for example, coping with the dissolution of a marriage than women. According to a recent study from the *Journal of Men's Health,* divorced men are more susceptible to heart disease, high blood pressure, and strokes than married men are—in addition to being 39 percent more likely to commit suicide and engage in risky behavior.

In the Bible we read that David and Jonathan's deep friendship and love for each other was so powerful that upon Jonathan's death, David gave this eulogy: "Your love for me was more wonderful than the love of women" (2 Sam. 1:26 NASB). That's quite a statement. There was nothing inordinate or depraved about that love; it was just a profound appreciation and care for the other.

I love that scene near the end of *A Good Day to Die Hard* (2013) when Bruce Willis's character and his son are loading up their guns outside of Chernobyl and preparing to go into the final showdown. Knowing they both might die, they try to say they love each other in a rough and tough way but have a hard time doing so. It's pretty funny, but touching.

It's important to realize as men we're to be strong in love and not harden our hearts to receiving or giving it. We're not to leave love for only women to express. Men set the tone of love or lack thereof in our world, again due to our position in the created order.

But how many of us get up out of bed thinking, *The most important purpose I have today is to show some love?* One of the reasons we don't naturally think we are a vital source of love in this world is, again, the way the media portray men. The news likes to portray us as troublemakers, and Hollywood as neglectful and insensitive, interested only in the ball game, sex, or World of Warcraft. Yet unless men love, there will be no lasting change for the better in our world. We can't ignore or discount men's capability and responsibility to love any longer.

It's men who get the direct command to love in marriage: "Husbands, love your wives, as Christ loved the church and gave himself up for her" (Eph. 5:25, ESV).

Wives aren't off the hook—they also need to love (Titus 2:4), but as the pioneering Christian counselor Jay Adams put boldly in his *Solving Marriage Problems,* "It's man's job to initiate and set the loving tone in the relationship." When husbands lead in love it's easier for wives to respond and carry on in that same spirit of affection to both their husbands and to the rest of the family.

Additionally it's men who set the tone for love in the church. Jesus said, "By this all people will know that you are my disciples, if you have love for one another" (John 13:35, ESV). All agree that this is the number-one characteristic defining Christians, the distinguishing mark and the top fruit of the Spirit. And the scripture is clear that men are to be the leaders in the church; therefore, they must certainly have the capacity to love and lead in love according to God's standards (Titus 1:5–6).

So be a lover even as you are a warrior. Make that the first goal again. The strong apostle Paul, who stood up for Christ before kings and officials, was beaten and thrown into prison, survived shipwrecks, and fought lions in the Roman arena, said, "If I have all faith so as to move mountains, but have not love, I am nothing" (1 Cor. 13:2 ESV).

Love is known by being shown. I'm sure you've heard "Love is a verb" or "Love is an action word." You can *say* you're loving, but unless you show it, the words ring hollow. The Bible declares God the Father loves us and he *showed* it by giving his Son to save us: "This is real love—not that we loved God, but that he loved us and sent his Son as a sacrifice to take away our sins" (1 John 4:10, NLT).

Scripture also says Jesus, the Son of God, loves us as well and *proved* it by sacrificing himself. Paul wrote, "I live by faith in the Son of God, who loved me and gave himself for me" (Gal. 2:20 ESV). E. A. Blum plainly states, "Love is the self-sacrificing desire to meet the needs of others, which finds expression in concrete acts." The bottom line is, if you love someone, you have to show it. I think that old Foreigner song, "I Wanna Know What Love Is," which is played on classic rock stations all the time, stated it quite profoundly: "I wanna know what love is, I want you to show me."

When I was a young pastor fresh out of seminary and working at a small rural church in Lancaster, Pennsylvania, I was pretty excited and eager about making program changes, bringing in new music, and preaching my heart out so we would grow. And the fine folks were considerate and willing to try, which was amazing since most were senior citizens! But for the first couple of months I sensed they were a little reserved and guarded, which is natural when a cocky new young pastor comes in. But then we had a workday at the church, and I was out there power washing and painting the building, which they were so fond of. The following Sunday I sensed a change of heart. They were much more open and committed to many of my suggestions for change to bring about growth. They had seen me display a true love for them and their church. (I guess their previous pastors didn't like to get their hands dirty!)

Author Gary Chapman, in his already classic book *The 5 Love Languages,* describes how we give and receive love in five main ways: through words of affirmation, quality time, gifts, acts of service, and physical touch. He says, "We need to find the primary ways our wives receive expressions of love and emphasize them—rather than express love in the way we ourselves like it shown." The point he makes is that love must be *expressed* in one way or another. Love is *outwardly performed.* As men we need to make deliberate efforts to portray love and endearment because love is *shown.*

Counselors agree: if you don't play with your kids and show affection so they know you love them, your influence, instruction, and discipline are much less effective and can even have adverse effects. Psychoanalyst Irving Bieber and later psychologist Elizabeth Moberly found in their studies that adult homosexual males tended to report having had less loving and more rejecting fathers than their heterosexual peers. And it is well known when fathers don't have healthy, loving relationships with their daughters, the girls often end up in the arms of their boyfriends seeking comfort and emotional support, resulting in sexual activity and teen pregnancy. Fathers and men need to show true love.

Part of the reason guys often fail in being loving is the confusion from the world about what sincere love looks like. We need to be reminded that it's not sex, even though we often call it "making love." Sex has to do with the desires of the body. One of the original Greek words translated "love" is *eros,* where our word *erotica* comes from. It refers to physical desire, which can be expressed in a loving or unloving manner.

We need to be reminded that love is not strictly about feelings or desires. The Greek word *psuche,* from which we get our word *psychology*—the study of the soul—is another aspect of love. Feelings come and go. Soul can and should be touched with affection from true love at times, but you and I know there are times we don't *feel* too much love and affection for someone, but we're still to love them.

True love is found deeper than soul and comes from the Spirit, making us able to do what's right and good, even when we don't feel like it. Yet another Greek term, *agape,* refers to love that is unconditional and lasting. It goes beyond the soul and feelings and comes from the heart, where your spirit and the Holy Spirit reside when you become born again. It's where God dwells. And the heart, as Joseph Stowell states, "is where we desire, deliberate, and decide." It's our disposition and motivating force in life, the air inside us. True love is generated here as we grow in our spiritual lives, making us able to show it even when we don't have a natural desire to do so, because with Christ in us, we have the others' best interest in mind.

The root of all sin is selfishness, being self-consumed and having an inward focus on ourselves. You can be in a marriage, and it's all about yourself. You can be active in the church, yet it's all with a self-promotion at the root. (The self loves to make itself look good in religiousness). You can even be a minister and underneath have it be driven by self-centered desires. We weren't created to be this way, but since the fall of man and the curse, we've turned to be self-serving and self-glorifying.

Real love is other focused. It's not thinking about self at all. Thank God he relieved us from this relentless bondage of selfishness by sending Jesus. His death and resurrection broke us out of it if you believe and receive him. Rejoice, we are now free to love!

True love is being committed to another's well-being regardless of the sacrifice or cost on our part. And it never stops (1 Cor. 13:8). Robert Heinlein defines it well: "Love is that condition in which the happiness of another person is essential to your own." Jesus displayed this pure love so powerfully to us.

True love requires strength and resolve, which is why I believe men are called to lead in it—and why Gandhi would rightly say, "A coward is incapable of love. It's the prerogative of the brave."

Wow! So where are we going to get the power and resource to show this kind of love? It's unnatural, especially in this dog-eat-dog world that wears down the heart. There's only one way: God. He's the source, for he is love! He is the deep sweet well of love that's bottomless.

"Whoever does not love does not know God, because God is love "(1 John 4:8, NIV). God doesn't just have love in his heart, he *is* love. It's the essence of who he is, his makeup, his Spirit, his heart.

This leads us to a crucial point about seeking to faithfully show love. When we continually know and realize the exhaustless love of God, and love him back, our spirits grow with strength and power to love others. When we are regularly refreshed and reminded of God's great love for us in Jesus Christ, we are renewed with energy to love others!

> You do not need anyone to write to you about the way Christians should love each other. God has taught you to love each other. (1 Thes. 4:9, God's Word Translation)
>
> We love because he first loved us. (1 John 4:19, ESV)
>
> I have loved you even as the Father has loved me. Remain in my love. (John 15:9, NLT)

Sister Sarah Young puts it eloquently in *Jesus Calling:* "As I [God] fill you with my love, you become a reservoir of love overflowing to the lives of other people." This is what it means to "love in the Spirit" (Col. 1:8, ESV), and it is the guiding principle and goal for the rest of our lives: to "be filled with the Spirit" (Eph. 5:18, ESV).

When we receive God's Holy Spirit upon salvation, we are given the power to love—agape style! The aged apostle Paul in his last letter said, "God gave to us a spirit not of fear but of power and love and self-control"(2

Tim. 1:7, ESV). We can love. It's in us. It's why Christians are really the only ones who can truly love. Yet the Spirit can become quenched, weak, and choked when we live sinfully, centered on our own lusts and selfish desires. For love to be strong in our lives, we must always seek to be renewed by the love of God in Christ Jesus and keep the Spirit flowing.

To make an impact for the kingdom of God, we will have to love those who don't deserve it, be kind to those who treat us harshly and with contempt, like that sassy teenager at home, flipping out because you grounded her for lying to you, or the coworkers who are angry and ignore you because they feel you're always judging them. Bearing up under ill treatment and still showing love defines spiritual leadership. But get this: we can't will it to happen by trying hard, even though we'd like to. Only through seeking to understand God's heart and dealings with us through Jesus and being refreshed by his great love, do we get the power to love consistently the way he does.

It is important to mention that love is shown by truth-telling. When we look at Jesus, the perfect example of love, we know scripture says he was "full of grace and truth" (John 1:14, ESV). We can't know and come into the love and grace of God without the truth of our sin and guilt before God.

Look at the famous woman at the well in John 4. You'll notice once she desired to have what Jesus had to offer, he pointed out her sin—not to condemn her, but to show her need to be saved from her sinfulness. When another woman caught in adultery was brought to him and he rescued her from being stoned, what did he say? "Neither do I condemn thee; go, and sin no more" (John 8:11 KJV). In our pursuit of being loving we can't forget the truth aspect! We must speak the truth or we will not be showing true love as "Love rejoices with the truth" (1 Cor. 13:6 NASB).

Paul wrote in 2 Thessalonians 2:10 about "those who are perishing, because they refused to love the truth and so be saved" (ESV). Love is not acceptance of evil. Many in today's world want to say Christians are not loving because they point out certain sinful lifestyles or declare something to be wrong. The world says that love is being tolerant and not judgmental. But that's not what Jesus did. He pointed out right and wrong.

God is love, as we know, but he is also holy, righteous, and just. These are the other parts of his character. If you want him and his love, you have to take all of him. He cares about right and wrongs. If God didn't uphold a righteous standard in the universe, Jesus' coming, his death, and resurrection, which brought much-needed forgiveness, would be meaningless. We don't see and know the love of God unless we're convicted of wrongs and understand our true state of guilt before him. From this comes the principle: true love occurs only where righteousness is sought after and upheld.

It's a fact: right and wrong are part of love. Understanding what God's expectations are according to his holy standard allows us to appreciate his love, grace, and forgiveness in Christ. . Bottom line: if you want God's love in your heart so you can love others, you have to also acknowledge and promote his righteousness. Not surprisingly, Jesus said regarding the end of this age before he returns, "Because lawlessness will be increased, the love of many will grow cold" (Matt. 24:12 ESV).

When we totally ignore right and wrong and fail in making a judgment on what's sin, (which is how the world defines love), we are actually desensitizing ourselves to the love of God, making ourselves less loving in the end. How ironic! Again, true love occurs only where righteousness is upheld. It may sound contradictory but it's not.

It's vital for us men, as aspiring spiritual leaders, to learn how to point out wrongdoing when needed, not just at home, or to fellow Christians, but also out in the world when possible. Though the world may accuse us of being judgmental, we need to remind ourselves speaking truth is really an act of love! True love wants what's best for someone and points him or her in the right direction for blessing.

But correction must be presented in the Spirit and tenderness of love. While speaking truth is a part of love, it's not love in itself. We can use truth to hurt and condemn others if we do it in the wrong way. It's not that we go around on the prowl, looking to point out other people's faults, nitpicking, and "declaring" truth.

Instead, we should see how sinful habits hurt people and distance them from God, and wanting happiness for them, we speak the truth. That's the spirit we go in. That's love. Just remember the tried-and-true saying: it's not what you say but how you say it. Truth must be presented in the spirit of love with humility. Then it can do its work in bringing others closer to God to experience his love.

Expressing love, which involves truth, is how we ARISE and stand as a true spiritual leader. Yet there is one particular expression of love that must be shown above all else that we'll end with.

You can't force someone to love you. The best you can do is strive to be someone worthy of loving.

Dipper Pines, *Gravity Falls*

"The most important thing in the world while you're on this side of eternity is that you learn to worship God. If you're going to do it for ever and ever, you ought to practice it now."

Leonard Ravenhill

Their hearts are far from me.

God

CHAPTER 13

LOVE FIRST LOVE FIRST

In one of my all-time favorite movies, *Bruce Almighty,* Bruce, played by Jim Carrey, gets use of God's power for a while. And after using it to help advance his career, along with getting some cheap thrills (like parting traffic as if Moses with the Red Sea to get to work on time), he finds that God's power can't help him with the one thing he really wants: to have his ex-girlfriend take him back and love him. At one point he tries to break the rules and mess with free will, stretching out his arms and commanding Grace, played by Jennifer Aniston, to love him. But it has no effect as she replies "I did" and walks away. (See it here: https://www.youtube.com/watch?v=6et2ZSodS0g.)

Often when we talk about love in Christian circles we go right to "love one another" and emphasize the need to show love one to another—as we did in the last chapter. "By this all people will know that you are my disciples, if you have love one for another" (John 13:35, ESV). Yet that is not the first act of love that we're responsible for. There's something, or rather someone, we gloss over all too quickly when we think about the need to show love—God! God wants us to love him first, because he desires it and deserves it.

Jesus said, "'Love the Lord your God with all your heart and with all your soul and with all your mind and with all your strength.' The second [commandment] is this: 'Love your neighbor as yourself'" (Mark 12:30–31, NIV). The first exercise of love we're to be concerned with is toward God. As a matter of fact, our love for God should be so strong that all other loves look like hate (see Luke 14:26).

It has been said God's one "weakness" is that he's looking for love. That's not an actual verse in scripture, but it does ring true. He's looking for love from us and went to great lengths to get it. He couldn't have given anything more to show us he loves us than giving his Son, and Jesus gave it all in his willingness to give his life to save us from perishing for all eternity.

But if you're like me, you're walking around all too often in a perpetual state of want! I'm sorry to say I don't give too much consideration for God's heart but am often driven to prayer and trying to do what pleases him because I want *blessing*. I want something from him. How often do we go before the Lord and say, "I just want to hang out with you because I really love you. I don't need anything right now; I just want to enjoy your presence, understand more of you, and tell you how much I love you"? If you're like me, not very often. The old English monk from the classic *The Cloud of Unknowing* states the goal well: "Lift up thine heart unto God with a meek stirring of love, and mean Himself and none of his goods."

If you're not able to get to this state of just being with God and telling him you love him at least sometimes, you're not knowing God the way he wants you to. And you might want to consider what kind of messages you are taking in about him. I get upset when preachers solely define love as obeying the commands of God. Yes, love will result in doing what God desires—but obedience is not the essence of love. You have to have love in your heart for God to consistently do what he wants.

There's a very revealing message in Revelation 2:1–7, where the Ephesian church was outwardly doing everything correctly, but they had lost their passionate love for Jesus. The Lord sensed it. They needed to get it back, or Jesus said their light and witness would go out. They reduced showing love for Jesus to keeping a strict standard they thought would please him. "I know your works, your toil and your patient endurance," he told them (Rev 2:2, ESV). They were busy, doing good things! But the "doing" became the focus and essence of their faith. The spirit of the Old Testament was creeping in.

Though the Law was supposed to generate and show how to love God and our neighbor (Deut. 6:5; Lev. 19:18), it only hardened human hearts due to the depravity of man's sinful nature. And it still does. You can't produce love for God himself (or anyone), when focusing solely on following his laws or a code of behavior derived from his laws. Paul reminds us, "We have been released from the law so that we serve in the new way of the Spirit, and not in the old way of the written code" (Rom. 7:6, NIV).

Some might object and quote what Jesus said, "Those who accept my commandments and obey them are the ones who love me" (John 14:21, NLT).

This is referring to the New Covenant, which is not based on law-keeping but on growing in grace and walking by faith in what Jesus has made us into now since his death and resurrection. It's loving one another by turning the other cheek and showing grace as Jesus taught. Those are the types of commands he was referring to in that verse.

Take care that your faith doesn't become defined as things you must do and not do for God. Because then instead of having a heart of love for all he's done, you're feeling good about yourself for all you've done! Then your love meter starts to drop.

It's better to be found in the grace of Christ for "he who is forgiven little, loves little" (Luke 7:47, ESV). Emphasis on the Law results in focusing on self, but grace gets you God-focused, praising and rejoicing in how good he is. So be careful what messages and teaching you are taking in about God. The author of Hebrews wrote, "It is good that the heart be established by grace" (Heb. 13:9, NKJV).

John Piper words it nicely: "We will love God to the degree that we recognize the magnitude of our sins and the immensity of God's grace to forgive them." I would include not only the forgiveness of sins, but also the immense value and all the blessings we have been given, now that we are made saints and one with Christ. We who were once rebels against him!

This is why Paul told Timothy, "Jesus came into the world to save sinners, of whom I am chief" (1 Tim. 1:15, NKJV). You don't expect that from the most prominent apostle in the New Testament. But he was showing how to remain empowered and changed by God's love. Experiencing God's goodness and mercy by being found before God accepted and forgiven, rather than trying to live under a strict moral code, is what changes the heart. Paul also wrote, "Are you unaware of his rich kindness, forbearance, and patience, that it is God's kindness that is leading you to repent?" (Rom. 2:4, ISV). These are the characteristics of love. It's God's love that changes the heart to repent, and want to do what pleases him.

You'll find that people who focus on doing the laws of God and approach God according to the spirit of the Old Testament are the least loving. They are focused more on themselves and maintaining their self-righteousness and begin to feel that God owes them because of the all the hard work they've done to maintain a rigid lifestyle. You can see this clearly in the prodigal son's older brother, whom Jesus spoke of to the Pharisees. When the prodigal came home, the father rejoiced and threw a party for him, but the older brother got mad and wouldn't attend. When the father entreated him to join the celebration, he said "What about me? Look at all I've done for you and you never threw a party for me" (see Luke 15).

To repeat the apt cliché, Christianity is not a religion, it's a relationship! Do you feel as though you're never doing enough for God? Or are you rejoicing in all that's been done for you in Christ and just looking for ways to show you love him back? It depends on the message that you're listening to about God. Seek the true message God has in Christ—it frees you up to love God first, and then others.

Notice the difference between Mary and Martha. Mary was sitting at the Lord's feet, listening to the mission and message of Jesus, understanding his work, and comprehending his beautiful person. Martha was serving and busy doing stuff—ministry stuff, getting ready to feed a bunch of hungry disciples—and complained that Mary wasn't contributing: "Lord . . . tell her to help me." And he tenderly said to her, "Martha, . . . Mary has chosen the better thing" (Matt. 10:40–42, NCV).

The Word of Christ will create love in your heart for God, which will bring about serving with a willing heart. Jesus wants us to serve, but he really wants us to serve out of love in response to his love. He's looking for a "cheerful giver" (2 Cor. 9:7, AMP), which comes from an overflowing heart filled with love, from understanding what he's about. It's why the apostle Paul said, "The love of Christ controls and compels us" (2 Cor. 5:14, AMP).

★★★

Mary gives us a great lesson as to how to exhibit love to God. This woman can teach us men something! What does she show us? After seeking and understanding Jesus and the Father's love, Mary showed her love and adoration to him by worshipping. She broke a very expensive jar of perfume over Jesus' head and feet and wiped them with her hair, (John 12:3). We need to get back to worshipping. It's how we exhibit love for God and find the power to serve. The saints of old always said, "Worship comes before service." It's important to God to hear you tell him you love him and how much you appreciate him.

> But a time is coming, and it is already here! Even now the true worshipers are being led by the Spirit to worship the Father according to the truth. These are the ones the Father is seeking to worship him. (John 4:23, CEV)

> Let us continually offer up a sacrifice of praise to God, that is, the fruit of lips that acknowledge his name. (Hebrews 13:15, ESV)

God deserves some uninterrupted attention, time when we're not caught up in doing anything else but worshipping and appreciating him. He's worth it. And we need to learn to take in preaching and teaching that's not *always* about "how it applies to ourselves," and "relevance to my life," but rather brings about worship for who God is, and what he's done. It's so refreshing to get our eyes off self and all we have to do, even good things, and just spend some time focusing on God and his Son.

Men, we're made to worship God. It's the business of heaven that starts now. And certainly we can do that in our prayer time before mentioning our requests or go out on a hike alone in nature with God and just meditate on him. But I do want to emphasize the importance of corporate worship. I know too many guys who believe in God, they are followers of Christ, but they just don't go to church anymore. If they do attend, they don't put much effort in the worship part of the service. Our kids need to see us worship! It shows them we love God, and teaches them how.

Too many Martha-minded pastors and preachers will say that it's with our lifestyles and service that we worship, and they'll base this idea on Romans. 12:1, where Paul told us to "present your bodies as a living sacrifice . . . which is your spiritual worship" (ESV). And that's true—the way we live and serve are a part of worship, but there is something else to be about to show our love and worship to God. It's doing nothing but together with other believers, focusing on him and pouring out our hearts in love and adoration for who he is and what he's done—the way Mary did.

Again it depends on what message you're taking in. As I mentioned back in chapter 5, when we study the Bible we shouldn't go straight to *How is this applied in my life?* or *What do I have to do?* Instead when we're in his Word we should look first for something that's amazing about God and Jesus and all they've done. Look for the many glorious aspects of their character, the perfection of their virtues, the marvelous applications and dimensions of salvation through the great wisdom of God, as well as his awesome love. Make it a priority when you're reading to look for something to magnify and worship him for, and jot them down on a pad. *Then* find applications for your life.

On Saturday night before you go to bed, go over the list you made of worshipful things about God. By doing so you're collecting a basket of thoughts to offer the Lord during worship the next day. Often we go to church to get; we feel dry and spiritually depleted from the week, and we go empty-handed. You can't worship that way! If you showed up back in ancient Israel at the tabernacle to worship without anything to offer and give the priest, they'd say, "Go home and come back when you have something"! We also should go to give love and appreciation to him for the things learned in our time of study, and by walking with him that week. And watch, the Lord will always give major blessings in return.

If you just can't seem to engage in worship where you go, look for a place where you can. Even more so, look for a place where you have a chance to participate in leading worship—someplace you can share some of the thoughts you've gathered or can pray, like the open worship service I mentioned in chapter 7. This can be difficult in a megachurch, where often they have tightly constructed programs. You may want to look for a smaller fellowship with more opportunity, because when you play a part in helping and leading others to worship, it will get you excited about worshipping God again.

Worship is our highest calling. Don't neglect it, either personal or corporate. It's the spark for all our Christian service and keeps us seeking after the wonderful person of God, and our calling to ARISE. We'll stay *after* God's heart and purposes, *read* and study the Word to reflect the Lord, *instruct* our families, our churches, and world, we'll show *strength* in faith and truth, and *exhibit love* if we seek to worship God.

Now you've risen up and have become the true man God intended with great purpose. Rejoice in it, and celebrate it! Crow and let all know that you are boldly standing against evil, declaring that the light has come, showing love, and speaking truth, all for the glory and love of God!

CPSIA information can be obtained
at www.ICGtesting.com
Printed in the USA
LVOW13s2011290317
528961LV00009B/12/P